CONTENTS

Copyright
Introduction
Preface
1. Introduction to Artificial Intelligence   1
2. What Is Traditional Programming?   4
3. From Traditional Programming to AI   8
4. Understanding Data: The Fuel of AI   12
5. Understanding Machine Learning   16
6. Generative AI: Creating New Content with AI   44
7. Evaluating AI Potential: Questions to Ask Before Starting   64
8. Building an AI Strategy   71
9. Choosing the Right AI Team   77
10. The Ethical and Regulatory Landscape   83
11. The Future of AI in Business   89
12. Glossary of Key AI Terms   96
13. AI Tools and Platforms for Beginners   106
14. AI in Manufacturing: Predictive Maintenance   113
15. AI in Logistics: Building a Smarter Supply Chain   120
16. AI in Agriculture: Optimizing Cow Breeding for Milking   127
17. Case Study Summaries and Key Takeaways   134

18. Conclusion: Why AI? A Roadmap for Decision-Makers   141
The Final Word   147
References   149

Copyright © 2024 PremKumar Kora

Artificial Intelligence: For the Decision Makers
PremKumar Kora & Rishi Kora

Copyright ©2024 Premkumar Kora and Rishi Kora
All rights reserved

This ebook edition is protected under copyright law. No part of this publication may be copied, reproduced, distributed, stored in a retrieval system, or transmitted in any form or by any means, whether electronic, mechanical, photocopying, recording, or otherwise, without prior written permission from the authors, except as permitted under applicable copyright laws.

The content in this ebook represents the combined expertise and interpretations of the authors. While every effort has been made to ensure the accuracy and relevance of the information presented, the authors and any associated publishers assume no liability for errors or omissions. The material provided is for informational purposes only and is not intended as a substitute for professional advice.

References to specific companies, organizations, products, or services are illustrative only. All trademarks, product names, and logos are the property of their respective owners and are used solely for identification purposes. Their inclusion does not imply sponsorship or endorsement of this publication.

ISBN: 9798302462527
First Ebook Edition December, 2025

Cover design: Rishi Kora
Interior design and layout: PremKumar Kora
Proofreader: Kavitha PremKumar

INTRODUCTION

In today's rapidly evolving business landscape, **Artificial Intelligence (AI)** has emerged as a transformative force, reshaping industries and unlocking unprecedented opportunities. Yet for many decision-makers, the concepts and applications of AI can feel distant, complex, or even intimidating. This book is designed to bridge that gap, empowering non-programmers in leadership roles to understand, evaluate, and implement AI effectively.

The Importance of Understanding AI in Business

AI is not just for tech giants or programmers—it's for everyone. Whether you're managing a manufacturing plant, overseeing logistics, or leading a dairy farm, AI offers practical solutions to everyday business challenges. From predicting equipment failures to optimizing supply chains and improving agricultural productivity, AI drives efficiency, innovation, and growth.

However, successful AI adoption requires more than enthusiasm; it demands informed decision-making. Leaders must understand **what AI is, how it works, and when to apply it**. This knowledge enables you to identify opportunities, avoid pitfalls, and align AI initiatives with your strategic vision. In a world where competitive advantage hinges on innovation, understanding AI is no longer optional—it's essential.

A Brief Overview of the Book's Structure and Main Themes

This book is structured to guide you step-by-step, from understanding foundational concepts to exploring real-world applications. It's divided into **seven parts**, each addressing a critical aspect of AI for decision-makers:

1. **Part I: The Foundations of AI and Traditional Programming**
    - Introduces the evolution from rule-based programming to AI-driven systems, highlighting the transformative power of data and machine learning.
2. **Part II: Core Concepts in AI**
    - Explains machine learning, generative AI, and their practical applications in solving real-world problems.
3. **Part III: AI for Decision Makers**
    - Focuses on evaluating AI's potential, building a strategy, and aligning AI projects with business goals.
4. **Part IV: Practical Insights for Implementing AI**
    - Provides actionable guidance on assembling the right team, navigating ethical challenges, and preparing for future AI trends.
5. **Part V: Practical AI Toolkit for Non-Programmers**
    - Includes a glossary of AI terms and an overview of beginner-friendly tools, enabling you to explore AI without technical expertise.
6. **Part VI: Industry Applications of AI**
    - Delves into specific use cases in manufacturing, logistics, and agriculture, with case studies that showcase AI's tangible impact.
7. **Part VII: Conclusion**
    - Wraps up with a roadmap for decision-makers, recapping key takeaways and offering actionable next steps to get started with AI.

How the Book is Organized for Readers' Benefit

This book is written with **non-technical leaders and decision-makers** in mind. It avoids heavy technical jargon, focusing instead on **clear explanations, practical examples, and actionable insights**. Here's how you can navigate the content:

- **Learn at Your Own Pace**: Each chapter builds on the last, allowing you to move sequentially or jump to sections most relevant to your needs.
- **Practical Focus**: Real-world case studies and industry-specific examples illustrate how AI solves common business challenges.
- **Hands-On Guidance**: The toolkit sections and step-by-step strategies ensure that you can apply what you learn directly to your organization.
- **Cross-Industry Relevance**: Examples span manufacturing, logistics, and agriculture, demonstrating AI's versatility and universal applicability.

This book is more than a guide—it's a roadmap to harnessing AI for growth, efficiency, and innovation. By the time you finish, you'll not only understand AI but also feel confident in leading its adoption within your organization. Whether you're just starting or looking to expand your AI initiatives, this book will equip you with the tools and insights to succeed in an AI-driven world. Let's get started!

PREFACE

The rapid evolution of Artificial Intelligence (AI) has fundamentally transformed the way we live, work, and do business. Yet, despite its growing influence, AI often remains misunderstood, particularly by decision-makers who are not immersed in technical fields. This gap inspired me to write this book. My goal is simple: to demystify AI and make it accessible to professionals who may not have a technical background but recognize the need to embrace AI as a critical tool for success.

As a consultant and practitioner in the AI space, I've witnessed firsthand how powerful AI can be in solving real-world problems —from optimizing manufacturing processes to improving logistics operations and enhancing agricultural productivity. I've also observed the hesitation and confusion that often accompanies the adoption of AI. Questions like "Where do I start?" or "How do I align AI with my business goals?" are common. This book is my attempt to address these questions and equip decision-makers with the knowledge they need to confidently lead AI-driven transformations.

Who is this book for?
This book is written for business leaders, managers, entrepreneurs, and professionals who are responsible for making strategic decisions but may feel overwhelmed by the technical jargon and complexities of AI. It's for individuals who don't need to write algorithms but want to understand how AI works, what it can do for their business, and how to implement it effectively.

What can you expect to gain?

By the end of this book, you'll have a clear understanding of AI's fundamental concepts. The book also provides guidance on evaluating AI's relevance, building a strategy, and avoiding common pitfalls. Most importantly, this book is not just about understanding AI—it's about action. My aim is to empower you with the knowledge and confidence to integrate AI into your business strategy, driving efficiency, innovation, and growth. Whether you're exploring AI for the first time or looking to expand your existing initiatives, this book is your roadmap to navigating the AI landscape.

Thank you for embarking on this journey with me. Together, let's unlock the transformative potential of AI and shape a smarter, more innovative future.

1. INTRODUCTION TO ARTIFICIAL INTELLIGENCE

Artificial Intelligence, or AI, is not just about robots or futuristic technology seen in movies; it's a transformative force shaping how we live, work, and make decisions today. At its core, AI refers to the ability of machines to mimic human intelligence—learning from experience, reasoning through data, and even making decisions.

1.1 What AI Really Means and Why It Matters

Think of AI as the next step in technological evolution. Just as the Industrial Revolution mechanized physical tasks, AI is revolutionizing cognitive tasks. It helps businesses analyze patterns, predict outcomes, and automate processes that once required human intuition. From personalized shopping recommendations to medical diagnoses, AI is already influencing countless aspects of daily life.

But why does this matter to you as a decision-maker? Because AI is not just a tool for engineers and data scientists; it's a strategic asset. Understanding how AI works and what it can achieve will empower you to make informed decisions that drive innovation and competitive advantage in your organization.

1.2 Why Non-Programmers Should Care About AI

It's easy to assume that AI is only for tech-savvy programmers or data scientists, but that's far from the truth. In fact, non-programmers—especially those in decision-making roles—play a crucial role in the successful adoption and implementation of AI. Here's why:

1. You Define the Problems AI Solves
   AI is a tool, and like any tool, its effectiveness depends on how it's used. As a decision-maker, you're in the best position to identify business challenges, prioritize goals, and determine where AI can deliver the most value.
2. You Bridge the Gap Between Business and Technology
   AI experts might know the technical aspects, but they often lack the context of your business needs. Your understanding of market trends, customer behavior, and operational priorities is essential for guiding AI projects in the right direction.
3. You Shape Ethical and Strategic Decisions
   AI raises critical questions about data privacy, bias, and transparency. As a leader, you'll need to ensure that AI systems align with your organization's values and long-term goals.
4. AI Impacts Your Industry—Ready or Not
   Whether you're in manufacturing, logistics, agriculture, or any other sector, AI is likely to disrupt your field. Staying ahead means understanding the basics of AI and preparing your team to adapt.

5. You Don't Need to Code to Lead
   Just as you don't need to be a mechanic to drive a car, you don't need to write algorithms to use AI effectively. What you need is a clear understanding of AI's capabilities, limitations, and potential applications in your business.

Artificial Intelligence is more than a buzzword; it's a game-changer for industries and decision-making processes. As a non-programmer in a leadership role, you have the unique opportunity to harness AI's power by defining its purpose, guiding its implementation, and ensuring its ethical use. This book will equip you with the knowledge and confidence to make AI a strategic ally, no matter your technical background.

2. WHAT IS TRADITIONAL PROGRAMMING?

2.1 Rule-Based Systems: How Computers Follow Instructions

Traditional programming, often referred to as rule-based programming, is the process of providing computers with explicit instructions to perform specific tasks. In this approach, programmers write step-by-step rules that a computer follows to achieve a desired outcome.

For example, let's consider a simple task: calculating the total cost of items in a shopping cart. In a traditional program, the instructions might look like this:

1. Add up the price of each item.
2. Apply any discounts or taxes.
3. Display the final amount.

The program does exactly what it's told—nothing more, nothing less. Every possible scenario must be anticipated and written as a rule. If an edge case arises (like a missing price or an unexpected type of discount), the program fails unless it has been explicitly programmed to handle it.

Traditional programming works well for:

- Structured tasks with clear inputs and outputs, such as payroll systems or inventory management.
- Repetitive tasks that don't require adaptation or learning.

However, these systems rely heavily on the programmer's foresight and can't go beyond their pre-defined rules.

2.2 Challenges in Complex Decision-Making

As tasks become more complex, traditional programming faces significant limitations. Here's why:

1. **Exponential Complexity**
   In dynamic systems like supply chain management or personalized customer experiences, the number of potential scenarios can skyrocket. Writing rules for every possible situation becomes impractical or even impossible.
2. **Inability to Adapt**
   Traditional systems are static. They operate based on predefined rules, which means they cannot learn from new data or adjust to changing conditions. For example, a rule-based system for fraud detection would struggle to identify new, unforeseen fraud patterns.
3. **Data Overload**
   Modern businesses generate massive amounts of data from sensors, customer interactions, and online platforms. Traditional programs cannot effectively process or extract insights from these vast, unstructured datasets.
4. **Limited Problem Solving**

Traditional systems are great at following instructions but poor at reasoning, recognizing patterns, or making predictions. Tasks requiring these capabilities—like diagnosing diseases or forecasting market trends—are beyond their reach.

2.3 Why Traditional Approaches Can't Keep Up

In today's world, businesses and industries face challenges that demand more flexibility, speed, and intelligence than traditional programming can provide. Here are the key reasons why traditional approaches fall short:

1. **Dynamic Environments**
   Consider a logistics company trying to optimize delivery routes in real-time. Factors like weather, traffic, and last-minute customer requests constantly change, making static rules insufficient.
2. **The Need for Personalization**
   Customers expect tailored experiences, whether it's product recommendations or personalized healthcare. Traditional programs struggle to deliver this level of customization.
3. **Competitive Pressures**
   As industries become more data-driven, organizations that rely solely on traditional programming risk being outpaced by competitors who leverage AI to make smarter, faster decisions.
4. **The Rise of Unstructured Data**
   Traditional programs are not designed to process unstructured data such as text, images, or audio. Yet, these types of data are increasingly important in areas like customer feedback analysis and facial recognition.

While traditional programming has been the backbone of computing for decades, its limitations in handling complexity, adapting to change, and leveraging vast amounts of data make it inadequate for many modern challenges. This is where Artificial Intelligence steps in—offering systems that can learn, adapt, and thrive in environments too dynamic for static rules.

In the next chapter, we'll explore how AI differs from traditional programming and why it's uniquely positioned to address today's most pressing challenges.

3. FROM TRADITIONAL PROGRAMMING TO AI

3.1 The Role of Data in Modern Systems

In the traditional programming paradigm, data was merely an input used to execute predefined instructions. In contrast, data is the lifeblood of Artificial Intelligence (AI). Modern systems rely on vast amounts of data to uncover patterns, make predictions, and continuously improve their performance. This shift has been made possible by advancements in storage, computing power, and connectivity.

1. **Data**
   AI systems don't function by following fixed rules; instead, they learn patterns and relationships from data. The more high-quality data you feed an AI system, the better it becomes at tasks like recognizing customer preferences, predicting equipment failures, or personalizing healthcare treatments.
2. Types of Data Used in AI
   o **Structured Data**: Organized in tables, such as sales

figures or inventory counts.
- o **Unstructured Data**: Images, videos, text, and audio that were traditionally difficult to analyze but are now invaluable to AI systems.
- o **Real-Time Data**: Streams of information from IoT devices, social media, or sensors, allowing AI to react dynamically to changing conditions.

3. **The Value of Data Diversity**
   AI thrives on diverse datasets. For instance, in a predictive maintenance application, combining historical repair logs with sensor data and environmental conditions provides a richer foundation for insights.

3.2 How AI Thinks Differently

AI fundamentally changes the way systems process information and solve problems. Unlike traditional programming, which relies on explicit instructions, AI systems learn from data to make decisions.

1. **Learning Instead of Following**
   Traditional programs follow "if-then" rules written by programmers. AI, on the other hand, uses algorithms to identify patterns in data. For example:
   - o A traditional program might flag a credit card transaction as fraudulent if it exceeds a certain amount.
   - o An AI system learns to recognize complex patterns of fraud based on historical data, such as unusual spending locations or timeframes.

2. **Adaptability**
   Traditional systems are static; they do what they were designed to do and nothing more. AI systems, however, adapt and improve over time. For example, an AI system analyzing customer behavior can refine its recommendations as new data flows in.

3. **Handling Complexity**
   AI excels at managing problems with multiple variables and high levels of uncertainty. For instance, in logistics, AI can consider real-time traffic data, fuel costs, and delivery deadlines simultaneously to optimize routes—something nearly impossible with rule-based programming.
4. **Decision-Making Without Explicit Rules**
   AI systems make decisions based on probabilities rather than deterministic rules. This allows them to operate effectively even in ambiguous or unpredictable scenarios.

3.3 Breaking Down AI Myths for Decision Makers

AI is often surrounded by hype and misconceptions, which can lead to unrealistic expectations or unnecessary fear. Let's address some common myths and set the record straight:

- Myth: AI Will Replace All Jobs
  Reality: AI is more about augmentation than replacement. While AI automates repetitive tasks, it creates opportunities for humans to focus on higher-value activities like strategy and innovation.
- Myth: AI Can Think Like Humans
  Reality: AI doesn't "think" or "understand" in the way humans do. It processes data and identifies patterns, but it lacks human qualities like intuition, creativity, and emotional intelligence.
- Myth: AI Systems Are Fully Autonomous
  Reality: Most AI applications today are tools that assist humans rather than independent systems. They require oversight to ensure they are aligned with business objectives and ethical standards.
- Myth: You Need a Massive Budget to Use AI
  Reality: While developing cutting-edge AI models can

be expensive, many affordable, ready-to-use AI solutions are available. Cloud platforms and AI-as-a-Service options make AI accessible to businesses of all sizes.
- Myth: AI Always Gets It Right
Reality: AI is not infallible. It depends on the quality of the data it's trained on. Biased or incomplete data can lead to flawed results, which is why human oversight is critical.

AI represents a paradigm shift in how we use technology to solve problems. By leveraging data, AI systems learn, adapt, and thrive in dynamic environments where traditional programming struggles. For decision-makers, understanding how AI thinks and debunking myths is crucial to harnessing its potential effectively.

4. UNDERSTANDING DATA: THE FUEL OF AI

4.1. Why Data Matters in AI

Data is the foundation of Artificial Intelligence. Unlike traditional programming, where rules are explicitly defined, AI systems learn from data to make decisions, predict outcomes, and generate insights. Without data, AI simply cannot function.

1. How Data Powers AI
   AI systems rely on data to:
   - Recognize patterns (e.g., identifying trends in customer behavior).
   - Make predictions (e.g., forecasting sales or detecting equipment failures).
   - Automate decisions (e.g., approving loans or suggesting products).

The more relevant and high-quality data an AI system has, the better its performance. For example, a predictive maintenance AI for manufacturing needs historical maintenance logs, sensor data, and environmental conditions to make accurate predictions.

2. Data as a Competitive Advantage
   Organizations that collect and leverage data effectively gain a competitive edge. They can make smarter, faster decisions and respond dynamically to market changes. Businesses without robust data strategies risk falling behind.
3. Garbage In, Garbage Out
   Poor-quality data leads to poor AI performance. If the data is biased, incomplete, or outdated, the AI system will produce unreliable or even harmful results. Data quality is as important as the quantity.

4.2. Types of Data: Structured, Unstructured, and Big Data

AI systems work with a variety of data types, each serving different purposes. Understanding these types helps decision-makers grasp how AI processes information.

1. Structured Data
   - Definition: Highly organized data stored in rows and columns, like spreadsheets or databases.
   - Examples: Customer information (names, ages, purchase history), financial records, inventory counts.
   - Use in AI: Structured data is often the starting point for AI models, especially in business analytics, fraud detection, and forecasting.
2. Unstructured Data
   - Definition: Data that doesn't follow a fixed format, making it harder to organize and analyze.
   - Examples: Emails, social media posts, images, videos, and audio recordings.
   - Use in AI: Unstructured data is a goldmine for AI, especially in areas like image recognition, sentiment analysis, and natural language processing.

3. Big Data
    - Definition: Extremely large datasets that traditional tools struggle to process due to their volume, velocity, and variety.
    - Examples: Real-time IoT sensor data, online streaming data, transaction records from millions of customers.
    - Use in AI: Big data allows AI systems to identify patterns and insights that smaller datasets might miss. For instance, analyzing global traffic data to optimize logistics routes.

4.3. Collecting, Cleaning, and Managing Data

The process of preparing data for AI is as crucial as the AI itself. Poorly managed data can derail even the best AI projects.

1. Collecting Data
    - Sources: Data can come from internal systems (e.g., CRM software, ERP systems), external sources (e.g., market research, public datasets), or real-time streams (e.g., IoT sensors).
    - Key Considerations:
        - Ensure data is relevant to the problem you're solving.
        - Verify that data collection complies with privacy regulations, like GDPR or CCPA.
2. Cleaning Data
    - Why It Matters: Raw data is often messy, with missing values, duplicates, or errors. Cleaning ensures the AI system receives accurate and reliable information.
    - Steps:
        - Remove duplicates to avoid skewed results.

- Fill missing values with appropriate estimates or exclude incomplete entries.
- Standardize formats (e.g., ensuring dates are in the same format across records).
  - Tools: Software like Python, R, or specialized ETL (Extract, Transform, Load) tools can automate much of this process.

3. Managing Data
   - Storage: Data must be stored securely and in a format that supports efficient analysis. Cloud platforms (e.g., AWS, Azure) are popular for their scalability.
   - Accessibility: Ensure the right people have access to the data while maintaining strict security protocols to prevent breaches.
   - Lifecycle Management: Not all data remains useful forever. Regularly review and archive old or irrelevant data to reduce clutter and improve efficiency.

Data is the backbone of AI. Understanding the types of data, their sources, and the processes for collecting, cleaning, and managing them is crucial for building effective AI systems. By investing in good data practices, businesses can unlock the full potential of AI, ensuring reliable insights and sustainable success.

5. UNDERSTANDING MACHINE LEARNING

5.1 The Concept of Learning from Data

Machine Learning (ML) is a subset of Artificial Intelligence that enables systems to learn from data rather than being explicitly programmed. Unlike traditional rule-based systems, which require every scenario to be coded, ML algorithms identify patterns and make predictions by analyzing data.

At its core, Machine Learning works like this:

1. Input Data: Provide historical data (e.g., customer purchase history or equipment performance logs).
2. Train the Model: The system analyzes the data, identifies relationships, and creates a model to predict or classify new data.
3. Make Predictions: Use the trained model to make decisions on unseen data, such as predicting customer preferences or detecting anomalies in machinery.

For example:

- Instead of programming rules for fraud detection (e.g.,

flagging transactions above $10,000), ML learns from past fraud cases to identify complex patterns, such as unusual spending locations combined with odd purchase times.

5.2 Types of Machine Learning

There are three main types of Machine Learning, each suited for different tasks.

Supervised Learning

Supervised learning is like teaching a child by showing examples. You provide the algorithm with input data (features) and the corresponding correct answers (labels), and the algorithm learns to predict the output for new, unseen inputs.

How It Works

1. Training Phase:
   o   The algorithm is fed with labeled data, such as images of cats and dogs, along with their labels (e.g., "cat" or "dog").
   o   It identifies patterns and relationships between the inputs and their respective outputs.
2. Prediction Phase:
   o   When presented with new, unlabeled data, the algorithm uses the learned patterns to predict the output.

Applications

- Regression (predicting continuous values):
  o   Predicting house prices based on size, location, and amenities.
  o   Forecasting sales or stock prices.
- Classification (categorizing data into discrete classes):
  o   Email spam detection.
  o   Diagnosing diseases (e.g., "positive" or "negative" test results).

Strengths
- Provides highly accurate results when trained on sufficient, high-quality data.
- Easy to evaluate with standard metrics like accuracy, precision, and recall.

Challenges
- Requires large volumes of labeled data, which can be expensive and time-consuming to generate.
- May struggle with bias and variance if the training data does not represent real-world conditions.

Unsupervised Learning

Unsupervised learning deals with unlabeled data, meaning the algorithm must find hidden patterns or structures without being explicitly told what to look for. This is similar to observing natural groupings in a dataset and categorizing them intuitively.

How It Works

1. Clustering:
   - Groups similar data points into clusters based on shared characteristics.
   - Example: Grouping customers with similar purchasing behaviors.
2. Dimensionality Reduction:
   - Reduces the number of features in a dataset while retaining its core information.
   - Example: Simplifying high-dimensional data for visualization or faster processing.

Applications
- Clustering:
  - Customer segmentation for targeted marketing campaigns.
  - Grouping similar products based on features.

- Anomaly Detection:
    - Identifying unusual patterns in network traffic to detect cyberattacks.
    - Spotting defective products in a manufacturing process.
- Recommender Systems:
    - Suggesting similar movies or books based on a user's preferences.

Strengths

- Can uncover hidden insights in large, unlabeled datasets.
- Requires no labeled data, making it cost-effective for initial explorations.

Challenges

- Results can be harder to interpret compared to supervised learning.
- Performance is highly dependent on the choice of algorithms and parameters.

Reinforcement Learning

Reinforcement Learning (RL) is inspired by how humans learn through trial and error. It involves an agent that interacts with an environment, makes decisions, and learns from the feedback it receives (rewards or penalties).

How It Works

1. The agent takes action in the environment.
2. The environment responds with a reward (positive feedback) or penalty (negative feedback).
3. The agent adjusts its strategy to maximize cumulative rewards over time.

Applications

- Robotics:
    - Teaching robots to perform complex tasks like

assembling components.
- Game Playing:
  - Training AI systems to play games like chess or Go at superhuman levels.
- Dynamic Systems:
  - Optimizing delivery routes in logistics based on real-time traffic data.
  - Controlling energy usage in smart grids.

Strengths

- Handles dynamic and complex environments effectively.
- Learns optimal strategies through exploration and feedback.
- Ideal for tasks requiring sequential decision-making.

Challenges

- Requires a well-defined environment and a reward system, which can be difficult to design.
- Computationally expensive, especially for large or complex environments.
- May not generalize well to unseen scenarios.

Comparison of Types

Aspect	Supervised Learning	Unsupervised Learning	Reinforcement Learning
Input Data	Labeled data with known outputs.	Unlabeled data with no predefined labels.	Environment with feedback (rewards/penalties).
Goal	Learn to map inputs to outputs.	Discover patterns or groupings.	Maximize cumulative rewards by learning optimal actions.
Common Algorithms	Linear regression, decision trees, SVM.	K-means clustering, PCA, DBSCAN.	Q-learning, deep Q-networks, policy gradients.
Applications	Spam detection, sales prediction.	Customer segmentation, anomaly detection.	Robotics, game AI, dynamic optimization.
Strengths	High accuracy with sufficient data.	Reveals hidden structures in data.	Excels in dynamic, real-time environments.

5.3 How Machine Learning

Solves Real Problems

Machine Learning shines in scenarios where traditional programming falls short, particularly in handling complexity and uncertainty. Here's how it solves real-world problems:

1. Recognizing Patterns
   ML excels at identifying patterns in large datasets. For example, it can analyze customer behavior to predict future purchases or detect irregularities in financial transactions.
2. Making Predictions
   ML models can forecast outcomes based on historical data. For instance, in predictive maintenance, ML can predict when a machine is likely to fail, preventing costly downtimes.
3. Automating Decisions
   ML can automate tasks like approving loan applications or recommending products, saving time and reducing human error.
4. Adapting Over Time
   Unlike static systems, ML models improve as more data becomes available, making them ideal for dynamic environments like e-commerce or traffic management.

5.4 Everyday Examples in Business

Machine Learning is not just for tech giants; it's already embedded in everyday business applications:

Retail and E-Commerce

Product Recommendations

One of the most well-known and effective applications of Machine Learning in retail and e-commerce is personalized product recommendations. This technology drives a significant portion of online sales for major platforms like Amazon, Netflix, and Spotify.

How It Works

1. Collecting Data
   Retailers collect user data such as:
   o   Browsing history (e.g., pages viewed, search queries).
   o   Purchase history (e.g., products bought previously).
   o   Interaction patterns (e.g., time spent on certain items or categories).
2. Analyzing Behavior
   Machine Learning models analyze this data to identify patterns. Two common approaches are:
   o   Collaborative Filtering:
   This method recommends products based on user similarities. For instance:
   - If User A and User B have similar purchase histories and User B buys Product X, the system suggests Product X to User A.
   o   Content-Based Filtering:
   This approach recommends products based on the attributes of items the user has interacted with. For example:
   - If a user buys running shoes, the system recommends related items like sports socks or gym bags.
3. Making Predictions
   The system uses the patterns it has learned to predict what products a user is likely to buy next and presents those items as recommendations.

Example in Action

- Scenario: An e-commerce customer purchases a smartphone.

- Recommendations:
  - Accessories like phone cases, chargers, or screen protectors (content-based filtering).
  - Products bought by other customers who purchased the same smartphone, like wireless headphones or a smartwatch (collaborative filtering).

Benefits

- Increased sales: Personalized recommendations can significantly boost conversion rates.
- Enhanced customer experience: Shoppers feel understood and catered to, increasing loyalty.
- Better inventory management: Retailers can promote items that are overstocked or complementary to trending products.

Dynamic Pricing

Dynamic pricing, also known as demand-based or time-based pricing, uses Machine Learning to automatically adjust the price of products based on a variety of factors.

How It Works

1. Collecting Data
   The system collects real-time and historical data on:
   - Product demand.
   - Competitor pricing.
   - Customer behavior (e.g., how many customers abandon their cart at a particular price).
   - External factors like seasonality, events, or weather.
2. Analyzing Data
   Machine Learning models analyze this data to

detect patterns, such as:
- How demand fluctuates at different price points.
- When competitors adjust their prices.
- Which customer segments are more price-sensitive.

3. Adjusting Prices

   Based on the analysis, the system updates prices dynamically to maximize revenue. For example:
   - Peak Demand: Prices increase when demand spikes (e.g., during Black Friday or a flash sale).
   - Low Demand: Discounts are applied to stimulate sales for products with slow-moving inventory.

Example in Action

- Scenario: A travel website selling airline tickets.
- Dynamic Pricing Implementation:
  - Prices increase as the departure date nears and seat availability decreases (higher demand).
  - Special discounts are applied during off-peak seasons to attract more buyers.

Benefits

- Increased profits: By charging higher prices during periods of high demand.
- Improved competitiveness: Adjusting prices in response to competitors' pricing.
- Better inventory management: Balancing supply and demand through pricing incentives.

Combining Product Recommendations and Dynamic Pricing

These two applications of Machine Learning often work hand-in-hand in e-commerce. For example:

- Scenario: A customer searches for hiking gear.

- System Response:
  - Recommends hiking boots, backpacks, and water bottles based on the user's previous purchases and browsing history.
  - Offers a limited-time discount (dynamic pricing) on items frequently bought together, incentivizing the customer to complete the purchase.

Machine Learning enables retailers and e-commerce platforms to:

Understand customer preferences: By analyzing large amounts of behavioral data.

Deliver personalized experiences: Through targeted recommendations.

Maximize revenue: Using dynamic pricing strategies. These applications not only enhance customer satisfaction but also drive profitability and efficiency for businesses in a competitive market.

Finance

Fraud Detection: Spotting Unusual Patterns in Transactions

Fraud detection is one of the most critical applications of Machine Learning in finance. By analyzing transaction data, Machine Learning models can detect patterns that indicate potential fraud, allowing financial institutions to act quickly and prevent losses.

How It Works

1. Collecting Data
   The system gathers a vast amount of transaction

data, including:
- Amount of the transaction.
- Location and time.
- Device used for the transaction.
- Historical transaction patterns of the user.

2. Training the Model
Machine Learning models are trained using both normal and fraudulent transaction data. The goal is to recognize patterns that differentiate legitimate transactions from fraudulent ones.

3. Real-Time Analysis
Once deployed, the model evaluates each transaction in real time. It calculates a fraud probability score by assessing:
- Deviation from user's typical behavior: For example, a transaction in a foreign country or an unusually high purchase amount.
- Known fraud patterns: Transactions resembling previously identified fraud cases.

4. Flagging Suspicious Transactions
If the model detects an anomaly or assigns a high fraud probability score, the transaction is flagged for further review or automatically declined.

Example in Action

- Scenario: A customer typically makes small purchases in their hometown. Suddenly, a large transaction is attempted from a foreign country using the same credit card.
- Fraud Detection System:
    1. The system identifies this as a significant deviation from the customer's historical spending pattern.
    2. It flags the transaction as suspicious and blocks it until further verification (e.g., confirming the transaction with the

customer via SMS).

Benefits

- Real-Time Detection: Prevents fraud before it occurs.
- High Accuracy: By learning from historical fraud patterns, the system reduces false positives and negatives.
- Cost Savings: Mitigates financial losses from fraudulent activities.

Credit Scoring: Analyzing Customer Profiles and Repayment Histories

Credit scoring evaluates a person's creditworthiness to decide whether they qualify for a loan or credit and, if so, on what terms. Machine Learning makes this process faster, more accurate, and more inclusive by analyzing a wide variety of data points.

How It Works

1. Collecting Data
   Machine Learning models use diverse data sources to assess creditworthiness, including:
   - Traditional factors: Income, employment history, and existing debt.
   - Behavioral data: Spending habits, payment patterns, and savings.
   - Alternative data: Social media activity, mobile phone usage, or utility payment history (in regions where formal financial records are scarce).
2. Training the Model
   The model is trained using historical data where outcomes are known (e.g., who repaid loans versus who defaulted). It learns relationships between various data points and the likelihood of repayment.

3. Predicting Creditworthiness
   When a new application is submitted, the system:
   - Analyzes the applicant's data against learned patterns.
   - Assigns a credit score or risk category.
   - Suggests loan terms, such as interest rate and amount, based on the predicted risk.

Example in Action

- Scenario: A young applicant with minimal credit history applies for a loan.
- Traditional Credit Scoring Challenges:
    1. Lack of sufficient data may lead to rejection despite their high earning potential and responsible behavior.
- Machine Learning-Based Credit Scoring:
    1. Analyzes alternative data, such as consistent utility bill payments and stable mobile phone usage.
    2. Recognizes patterns indicating responsible financial behavior.
    3. Approves the loan with a moderate interest rate based on the predicted low default risk.

Benefits

- Fairer Assessments: Includes alternative data sources, enabling underserved populations (e.g., young adults, new businesses) to access credit.
- Dynamic Updates: Continuously adapts to changes in customer behavior.
- Improved Accuracy: Reduces the risk of approving high-risk borrowers or rejecting low-risk ones.

Combining Fraud Detection and Credit Scoring

These applications often work together in financial institutions. For example:

- Scenario: A bank processes a loan application for a customer who has flagged transactions in their account history.
- System Response:
  1. Fraud detection flags recent suspicious activity, prompting the bank to investigate further.
  2. Credit scoring evaluates the customer's overall risk profile, balancing the flagged behavior with long-term repayment patterns.
  3. A decision is made to approve or reject the loan based on combined insights from both systems.

Fraud Detection: Prevents financial losses by identifying unusual patterns in real-time.

Credit Scoring: Enhances fairness and accuracy by leveraging diverse data points and advanced algorithms. Together, these applications showcase the power of Machine Learning in improving efficiency, accuracy, and customer experience in the financial sector.

Healthcare

Diagnosing Diseases and Predicting Patient Outcomes

Machine Learning (ML) has revolutionized healthcare, particularly in diagnosing diseases and predicting patient outcomes. By analyzing vast datasets, including medical images and health records, ML provides faster, more accurate insights, aiding in early detection, personalized treatment plans, and better patient outcomes.

Diagnosing Diseases from Medical Images

One of the most impactful applications of ML in healthcare is in medical imaging. By analyzing X-rays, MRIs, CT scans, and other medical images, ML models can detect anomalies, such as tumors or fractures, with high accuracy.

How It Works

1. Data Collection
   - Thousands of annotated medical images (e.g., X-rays with labels indicating "cancer" or "no cancer") are collected to train the ML model.
   - Data includes various conditions, imaging types, and patient demographics to ensure robustness.
2. Model Training
   - The model learns to identify patterns associated with specific diseases by analyzing pixel-level details and features (e.g., size, shape, or texture of a tumor).
   - Deep learning techniques, such as Convolutional Neural Networks (CNNs), are often used for image analysis.
3. Prediction
   - When a new, unseen medical image is input, the model predicts the likelihood of the disease (e.g., "90% chance of lung cancer").
4. Validation
   - Predictions are validated by cross-referencing with a physician's diagnosis to ensure reliability.

Example in Action

- Scenario: Detecting lung cancer in chest X-rays.
- Traditional Method: A radiologist manually examines hundreds of X-rays daily, which can lead to fatigue and occasional oversight.
- Machine Learning Solution:

1. An ML system analyzes the X-rays for early signs of lung cancer.
2. It flags suspicious images for further review by the radiologist.
3. The system highlights areas of concern (e.g., unusual nodules) for focused attention.

Benefits

- Early Detection: Identifies diseases at earlier stages, improving treatment outcomes.
- Efficiency: Reduces the workload of healthcare professionals by automating routine checks.
- Consistency: Minimizes human error, ensuring reliable analysis across cases

Predicting Patient Outcomes Based on Health Records and Treatment Plans

ML also excels in predicting patient outcomes, such as recovery likelihood, hospital readmission risk, or response to a specific treatment. These predictions help doctors personalize care and allocate resources more effectively.

How It Works

1. Data Collection
   - Data is gathered from electronic health records (EHRs), including:
     - Patient demographics (age, gender).
     - Medical history (chronic conditions, past treatments).
     - Lab results and vitals (blood pressure, cholesterol levels).
     - Treatment details (medications, procedures).
2. Model Training
   - The ML model is trained on historical data

where outcomes are already known (e.g., patients who recovered, were readmitted, or experienced complications).
  - It identifies patterns and relationships between variables that influence outcomes.
3. Outcome Prediction
  - For new patients, the model predicts:
    - Risk of complications (e.g., infection after surgery).
    - Recovery time based on treatment options.
    - Probability of hospital readmission.

Example in Action

- Scenario: Predicting recovery after a heart attack.
- Traditional Method: Physicians rely on general guidelines and subjective judgment to estimate recovery times.
- Machine Learning Solution:
  1. An ML system analyzes the patient's health records, including vitals, past conditions, and current treatment plans.
  2. It predicts a recovery timeline and highlights potential risk factors (e.g., poor adherence to medication, high stress levels).
  3. The system recommends tailored interventions, such as increased follow-up frequency or lifestyle modifications.

Benefits

- Personalized Care: Tailors treatment plans to individual patient needs, improving outcomes.
- Proactive Interventions: Flags high-risk patients for closer monitoring.
- Resource Optimization: Helps hospitals allocate resources more efficiently (e.g., ICU beds, staff).

Combining Disease Diagnosis and Outcome Prediction

These applications often work in tandem for holistic healthcare solutions.

Example: Breast Cancer

- Disease Diagnosis:
    - An ML model detects breast cancer in mammograms with high accuracy, identifying tumors invisible to the naked eye.
- Outcome Prediction:
    - Another model predicts the patient's response to chemotherapy based on genetic markers, tumor size, and health history.
- Integrated Care:
    - Together, these insights help oncologists choose the most effective treatment plan while preparing for potential side effects or complications.

1. Diagnosing Diseases: Machine Learning models analyze medical images to detect conditions like cancer with speed and precision.
2. Predicting Outcomes: By examining health records and treatment plans, ML provides insights into recovery timelines and potential risks.
3. Real-World Impact: These tools enhance early detection, enable personalized care, and improve healthcare efficiency, ultimately saving lives and resources.

Machine Learning is transforming healthcare into a data-driven field where decisions are faster, more accurate, and tailored to individual needs.

Manufacturing

Predictive Maintenance and Quality Control

Machine Learning (ML) has significantly improved efficiency in manufacturing, particularly through predictive maintenance and quality control. These applications minimize downtime, reduce waste, and ensure consistent product quality, enabling manufacturers to save costs and enhance operational reliability.

Predictive Maintenance: Avoiding Costly Equipment Failures

Predictive maintenance uses ML to monitor equipment performance in real-time and predict when a machine is likely to fail. This approach shifts maintenance from a reactive or scheduled model to a proactive one, reducing downtime and extending equipment lifespan.

How It Works

1. Data Collection
   - Sensors installed on machines collect data, such as:
     - Temperature, vibration, and noise levels.
     - Usage hours and load conditions.
     - Historical maintenance logs and failure records.
2. Model Training
   - ML models are trained on historical data to learn patterns that precede equipment failures (e.g., increased vibration before a motor breakdown).
   - Algorithms, such as time-series analysis and anomaly detection, are commonly used.
3. Real-Time Monitoring and Prediction
   - The ML model continuously monitors real-time

sensor data.
- When the model detects patterns indicative of potential failure, it raises an alert, allowing maintenance teams to act before the breakdown occurs.

Example in Action

- Scenario: Predictive maintenance for industrial motors in a factory.
- Traditional Method: Motors are maintained every six months regardless of their condition, leading to:
    1. Over-maintenance of some motors (wasting resources).
    2. Unexpected failures in others that degrade faster than expected.
- Machine Learning Solution:
    1. Sensors track motor data, such as vibration and heat levels, 24/7.
    2. The ML model identifies abnormal patterns, like a gradual rise in vibration, which often indicates bearing wear.
    3. It predicts that the motor will fail within two weeks if not serviced.
    4. Maintenance is scheduled immediately, avoiding unplanned downtime.

Benefits

- Cost Savings: Prevents expensive emergency repairs and reduces over-maintenance costs.
- Increased Efficiency: Minimizes production interruptions caused by unexpected equipment failures.
- Longer Equipment Lifespan: Proactive maintenance reduces wear and tear.

Quality Control: Detecting Defects in Production Lines

Machine Learning enhances quality control by automating defect detection in production lines. ML models analyze visual or sensor data to spot defects faster and more accurately than human inspectors.

How It Works

1. Data Collection
   - High-resolution cameras or sensors capture data about products on the production line.
   - This includes:
     - Surface appearance (scratches, dents).
     - Dimensions and tolerances.
     - Internal quality (e.g., X-rays for detecting internal flaws).
2. Model Training
   - The ML model is trained using labeled images or sensor data of both defective and defect-free products.
   - It learns to recognize even subtle deviations that indicate a defect.
3. Real-Time Defect Detection
   - The model processes images or sensor data in

real time.
- When a defect is detected, it flags the product and removes it from the production line or triggers an alert.

Example in Action

- Scenario: Quality control for smartphone manufacturing.
- Traditional Method: Human inspectors manually check thousands of phones for defects, leading to:
  1. Inconsistent detection rates due to fatigue.
  2. Slow production line speeds.
- Machine Learning Solution:
  1. Cameras capture images of smartphone screens and casings as they pass on the conveyor belt.
  2. The ML model identifies imperfections, such as tiny cracks or uneven alignment, with a 99% accuracy rate.
  3. Defective units are automatically removed for rework or recycling.

Benefits

- Accuracy: ML identifies defects that may be too subtle for human eyes to catch.
- Consistency: Unlike humans, ML systems don't tire or lose focus.
- Speed: Enables faster inspection, maintaining high production rates without compromising quality.

Combining Predictive Maintenance and Quality Control

In modern factories, these two applications often work together to optimize production processes.

Example: Automotive Manufacturing

- Predictive Maintenance:
  - Sensors monitor assembly line robots, predicting when components like robotic arms or conveyor belts need servicing. This prevents delays in vehicle production.
- Quality Control:
  - Cameras inspect car bodies for paint imperfections or misaligned parts. Defects are flagged immediately, ensuring only high-quality vehicles reach the market.

Integrated Benefits

- Reduced downtime leads to uninterrupted production.
- Automated quality checks ensure consistent output, enhancing customer satisfaction.
- Combining these systems creates a fully optimized, smart manufacturing environment.

Key Takeaways

1. Predictive Maintenance: ML helps manufacturers avoid costly breakdowns by predicting equipment failures before they happen.
2. Quality Control: ML automates defect detection, ensuring consistent product quality and faster production rates.
3. Real-World Impact: These applications reduce costs, improve operational efficiency, and boost customer satisfaction, making them essential for modern manufacturing facilities.

Logistics

Optimizing Delivery Routes and Inventory Management

Logistics is one of the industries most transformed by Machine Learning (ML). From optimizing delivery routes to forecasting demand for better inventory management, ML provides efficiency, cost savings, and customer satisfaction.

Optimizing Delivery Routes Using Real-Time Traffic Data

Efficient route optimization is critical for logistics companies to reduce delivery times, save fuel, and improve customer satisfaction. Machine Learning enables dynamic route planning by analyzing real-time data and adapting to changing conditions.

How It Works

1. Data Collection
   - Data sources include:
     - GPS data from delivery vehicles.
     - Real-time traffic conditions.
     - Weather forecasts.
     - Delivery deadlines and priorities.
2. Model Training
   - Historical data on past deliveries, including delivery times, route efficiency, and delays, is used to train the ML model.
   - The model learns to balance multiple factors, such as traffic congestion, fuel consumption, and delivery time windows.
3. Real-Time Optimization
   - When a delivery is initiated, the ML system analyzes current conditions and calculates the most efficient route.
   - If traffic patterns or weather conditions change, the model updates the route dynamically and communicates it to the driver.

Example in Action

- Scenario: A courier company delivering parcels across a busy metropolitan area.
- Traditional Method: Drivers follow pre-planned routes, often based on static maps that don't account for traffic or other dynamic factors.
- Machine Learning Solution:
    1. The ML model analyzes real-time traffic data and delivery locations.
    2. It predicts potential delays, such as traffic jams, and reroutes drivers to avoid congested areas.
    3. For high-priority parcels, the system allocates resources, such as assigning faster routes or additional drivers if delays are unavoidable.

Benefits

- Reduced Delivery Times: Real-time adjustments ensure faster deliveries, enhancing customer satisfaction.
- Fuel Savings: Optimized routes reduce unnecessary mileage and fuel consumption.
- Adaptability: The system adjusts to unexpected events, such as road closures or accidents, minimizing disruptions.

Inventory Management by Forecasting Demand and Avoiding Stockouts

Inventory management is another crucial area where Machine Learning delivers significant benefits. By forecasting demand, ML ensures optimal stock levels, preventing both overstocking and stockouts.

How It Works

1. Data Collection
   o   Relevant data includes:
       ▪ Historical sales data.
       ▪ Seasonality trends.
       ▪ External factors like economic indicators, promotions, or holidays.
       ▪ Supply chain information, such as lead times and supplier reliability.
2. Model Training
   o   ML models analyze historical and real-time data to identify patterns in demand.
   o   They account for variables like seasonality (e.g., higher demand during the holiday season) and external events (e.g., a sudden surge in demand for medical supplies during a pandemic).
3. Demand Forecasting
   o   The model predicts future demand for each product at different locations.
   o   It identifies trends (e.g., increasing demand for winter clothing as temperatures drop) and adjusts inventory levels accordingly.
4. Replenishment Planning
   o   The system ensures stock is replenished at the right time and in the right quantities, reducing holding costs and avoiding stockouts.

Example in Action

- Scenario: A retail chain managing inventory for its network of stores.
- Traditional Method: Inventory levels are replenished based on static reorder points, often leading to either overstocking (wasted resources) or stockouts (lost sales).
- Machine Learning Solution:
    1. The ML model forecasts demand for each

product at each store based on historical sales, promotions, and local events.
2. It predicts that demand for sunscreen will spike in coastal stores during a holiday weekend but remain stable in inland locations.
3. Inventory is adjusted dynamically, ensuring coastal stores are well-stocked without overstocking other locations.

Benefits

- Cost Savings: Optimizing inventory reduces storage costs and minimizes wastage.
- Improved Customer Satisfaction: Ensures products are always available when customers need them.
- Efficiency: Automates complex decisions about when and where to replenish stock.

Combining Delivery Optimization and Inventory Management

These two applications often work together in an integrated logistics system.

Example: E-commerce Giant

- Delivery Optimization:
    - Orders are routed dynamically to the nearest warehouse and delivered using the most efficient routes based on real-time traffic.

- Inventory Management:
    - The system predicts demand for products at specific locations, ensuring warehouses closest to major cities are well-stocked, reducing delivery times and costs.
- Integrated Outcome:
    - Customers receive their orders faster, and the company reduces operational costs through streamlined inventory and delivery management.

1. Route Optimization: Machine Learning minimizes delivery times and fuel costs by dynamically adjusting routes based on real-time traffic and weather conditions.
2. Inventory Management: By forecasting demand and planning replenishments, ML prevents stockouts and overstocking, optimizing operational efficiency.
3. Real-World Impact: Together, these ML applications help logistics companies reduce costs, improve efficiency, and deliver a superior customer experience, making them indispensable in modern supply chain management.

Machine Learning is a transformative technology that enables systems to learn from data, adapt to new conditions, and solve complex problems. With applications ranging from personalized marketing to predictive maintenance, ML is becoming an essential tool for businesses across industries.

6. GENERATIVE AI: CREATING NEW CONTENT WITH AI

Generative AI is a groundbreaking subset of Artificial Intelligence that focuses on creating new, original content—whether text, images, audio, or video—that mimics the patterns of the data it was trained on. It's reshaping industries by enabling creative processes, automating content generation, and simulating real-world scenarios.

A *foundation model* is a large, pre-trained AI model developed using vast datasets and advanced architectures, such as transformers. These models are designed to perform a wide range of tasks, from language understanding to image generation, without needing to be retrained from scratch for each specific use case. Examples include OpenAI's GPT, Google's BERT, and DALL-E. Their versatility allows businesses to fine-tune them for specialized applications, saving time and resources.

Large Language Models (LLMs) are a *subset of foundation models* specifically designed for processing and generating human language. While foundation models are general-purpose and trained on diverse datasets that include text, images, or even audio, LLMs focus primarily on natural language tasks like translation, summarization, text generation, and question-answering.

LLMs, such as OpenAI's GPT series or Google's Bard, are built on architectures like transformers and trained on vast amounts of textual data. Their capabilities, including understanding context and generating coherent responses, make them a powerful tool for language-related applications. As part of the broader foundation model family, LLMs inherit the flexibility and adaptability of these general-purpose models, but they specialize in excelling at tasks involving human language.

6.1 What is Generative AI?

Generative AI refers to AI systems capable of producing new data that resembles the original training data. Unlike predictive models that answer questions like *"What will happen next?"* generative models answer, *"What could be created?"*

Key Characteristics

- Creative Output: Generates text, images, audio, or even 3D models.
- Data-Driven Creativity: Learns from existing data to generate similar but unique outputs.
- Applications: From writing stories and creating artwork to simulating environments for training autonomous systems.

How It Works

- Generative AI models learn patterns, structures, and styles in data during training.
- After training, the model uses these insights to generate new content, often tailored to specific requirements.

6.2 Types of Generative Models:

GANs, Transformers & Beyond

1. Generative Adversarial Networks (GANs)
   - What They Are: A type of neural network consisting of two components:
     - Generator: Creates new data.
     - Discriminator: Evaluates the data and provides feedback to improve the generator.
   - Use Cases: Generating realistic images (e.g., deepfakes), creating artwork, and simulating data for training models.
   - Example: GANs can generate lifelike images of people who don't exist or synthesize new product designs.

2. Transformers
   - What They Are: A neural network architecture designed to process sequential data like text, enabling context-aware generation.
   - Use Cases: Writing essays, generating code, summarizing text, and creating conversational agents.
   - Examples:
     - GPT (Generative Pre-trained Transformer): Powers chatbots like ChatGPT and generates human-like text.
     - DALL-E: Creates images from text descriptions.

3. Variational Autoencoders (VAEs)
   - What They Are: Neural networks designed to encode data into a compressed form and then decode it back into an approximate representation.
   - Use Cases: Generating images, reconstructing incomplete data, and simulating environments.

4. Diffusion Models
   - What They Are: These models create data by learning how to gradually transform noise into meaningful outputs.
   - Use Cases: High-quality image generation, such as photo-realistic visuals and 3D modeling.

6.3 Examples of Generative AI in the Real World

1. Text Generation
   - Example: Generative AI can draft emails, write articles, or create conversational responses in chatbots.
   - Real-World Use:
     - Automating content creation for marketing campaigns.
     - Writing personalized product descriptions for e-commerce websites.
2. Image Creation
   - Example: Tools like DALL-E or MidJourney create unique images based on textual descriptions.
   - Real-World Use:
     - Designing visual assets for advertisements.
     - Generating realistic images for games and movies.
3. Music and Audio Synthesis
   - Example: AI can compose original music or mimic a specific artist's style.
   - Real-World Use:
     - Creating background music for videos.

- Voice cloning for personalized audio assistants.

4. Simulation and Prototyping
    - Example: Generating synthetic data for training autonomous vehicles or testing software.
    - Real-World Use:
        - Training autonomous drones in virtual environments.
        - Generating synthetic medical data for research while preserving patient privacy.

5. Video and Animation
    - Example: Generating lifelike animations for characters in video games or virtual reality.
    - Real-World Use:
        - Enhancing storytelling in media and entertainment.
        - Creating virtual influencers or avatars.

6.4 When and Why Should You Use Generative AI

Generative AI shines in diverse applications where creativity, efficiency, personalization, and resource optimization are essential. Let's break down each scenario to illustrate when and why it's effective:

1. Creativity is a Priority:

Generative AI is a game-changer for creative industries, where producing unique and innovative content is essential.

- Use Case Examples:
    - Art and Design:
        - Tools like DALL-E or MidJourney can generate unique artwork, product designs, or advertising visuals based on prompts.

- For example, a company launching a new sneaker line could use generative AI to create multiple design prototypes in various styles.
  - Storytelling:
    - Writers and filmmakers can use tools like GPT models to generate ideas, scripts, or entire stories.
    - For example, a scriptwriter could input a prompt like "A suspense thriller set in a dystopian future," and the AI would generate a draft to refine.
  - Game Development:
    - Generative AI can create game assets, such as characters, landscapes, or soundtracks.
    - For instance, game developers could use AI to generate realistic virtual worlds quickly.
- Why Use It:
  - To produce innovative ideas at scale.
  - To assist human creators by providing inspiration and drafts.

2. Automation Saves Time:

An Example in Marketing Content Creation

One of the most time-consuming tasks in marketing is content creation. From drafting social media posts to writing blog articles and product descriptions, these repetitive yet essential activities can be automated effectively using generative AI. This saves time and allows marketing teams to focus on strategy and creativity.

Example Scenario: An E-Commerce Company

Problem: An online retailer wants to scale its operations by expanding its product catalog from 1,000 to 10,000 items. Writing product descriptions for each item manually would take weeks and require a large team of content writers, increasing costs and delaying the product launch.

Traditional Method

- A team of writers is tasked with creating product descriptions.
- Each writer spends 10–15 minutes per description, which means completing 10,000 descriptions would take approximately 2,500 work hours.
- Challenges:
    - High labor costs.
    - Risk of inconsistent tone and quality.
    - Delays in getting products live on the platform.

Generative AI Solution

- The company uses a generative AI tool like OpenAI GPT or Jasper AI to automate product description writing.

How It Works:

1. Data Input:
    - The retailer provides product details such as name, category, features, dimensions, and intended use.
    - Example Input for a Running Shoe:
        - Name: SpeedRun Pro 3000
        - Features: Lightweight, breathable mesh, durable rubber sole.

- Use: Trail running.

2. AI Content Generation:
    - The AI generates descriptions tailored to the retailer's tone and style guidelines.
    - Example Output:
        - "Experience the ultimate comfort and performance with the SpeedRun Pro 3000. Designed for trail running, these lightweight shoes feature breathable mesh for ventilation and a durable rubber sole for superior grip on rugged terrain. Whether you're conquering mountain paths or urban streets, these shoes will keep you moving with confidence."

3. Customization:
    - Marketers can review and tweak the AI-generated descriptions for specific campaigns or SEO optimization.

Results

- Time Savings:
    - The AI generates 10,000 descriptions in hours instead of weeks.
    - Writers focus on reviewing and enhancing the output rather than starting from scratch.
- Cost Reduction:
    - The company avoids hiring additional content creators or overburdening the existing team.
- Consistency:
    - Ensures all descriptions maintain a cohesive tone and style, reinforcing the brand's identity.

- Scalability:
  - The company can add thousands of products in the future without worrying about content creation bottlenecks.

Other Applications in Marketing Automation

1. Social Media Posts:
   - AI generates engaging posts tailored for different platforms (e.g., Instagram, LinkedIn, Twitter).
   - Example: "Step into comfort! Our new SpeedRun Pro 3000 is now available. Perfect for trail running enthusiasts. Shop now!"
2. Ad Copy:
   - AI creates short, compelling ad headlines and descriptions for Google Ads or Facebook Ads.
   - Example: "Run Faster, Longer: Lightweight trail running shoes built for adventure. Get yours today!"
3. Email Campaigns:
   - Personalized email drafts tailored to customer segments.
   - Example:
     - Subject Line: "Conquer the Trails with SpeedRun Pro 3000!"
     - Body: "Hi [Customer Name], Ready to take your trail running to the next level? Our SpeedRun Pro 3000 is designed for performance and durability. Order now and get 20% off your first purchase!"
4. Blog Content:
   - AI generates long-form articles on topics

relevant to the business.
- Example: "5 Reasons Why Trail Running is the Ultimate Fitness Activity."

Key Benefits of Generative AI for Automation

1. Speed: Completes tasks in minutes that would take humans days or weeks.
2. Cost Efficiency: Reduces reliance on large teams for repetitive tasks.
3. Scalability: Handles increasing workloads seamlessly.
4. Consistency: Ensures brand messaging is uniform across all content types.

By automating repetitive tasks like content creation, generative AI enables businesses to save time, reduce costs, and scale operations effectively. In the case of marketing, AI-powered tools not only streamline the process but also maintain creativity and consistency, making them indispensable for modern businesses.

3. Personalization is Key:

Generative AI excels in creating personalized user experiences by analyzing data about user behavior, preferences, and needs. It delivers tailored recommendations, responses, or content, improving engagement, satisfaction, and loyalty.

Example Scenario: E-Commerce Platform for

Personalized Product Recommendations

Problem: An online retail platform wants to increase customer engagement and boost sales by offering highly personalized product recommendations. However, manually curating recommendations or using static rules (e.g., "customers who bought X also bought Y") results in generic suggestions that don't cater to individual preferences.

Traditional Method

- The platform uses static recommendation rules:
  o Recommends popular products based on category or general trends.
  o Relies on a simple "frequently bought together" algorithm.
- Challenges:
  o Recommendations feel impersonal and irrelevant to individual customers.
  o Limited ability to adapt to evolving user behavior or preferences.

Generative AI Solution

The platform implements a Generative AI-powered recommendation system to personalize user experiences in real time.

How It Works:

1. Data Collection:
   o The platform collects data from various touchpoints, including:
     - Browsing history (e.g., products viewed).
     - Purchase history (e.g., previous orders).

- Search queries (e.g., "sports shoes under $100").
- Demographics and preferences (e.g., gender, age, location).

2. AI Analysis:
   - A machine learning model (e.g., a transformer-based recommendation system) processes this data to understand user preferences and predict interests.
3. Personalized Recommendations
   - The AI generates real-time suggestions for each user:
     - Product suggestions on the homepage.
     - Dynamic bundling of related products (e.g., running shoes paired with socks and fitness trackers).
     - Targeted email campaigns with curated product lists based on recent activity.

Example in Action

- Customer A:
  - Browses for hiking boots and water bottles.
  - The AI recommends:
    - A high-quality backpack designed for hikers.
    - A portable water purifier for outdoor enthusiasts.
    - A discounted bundle of hiking boots and trekking poles.
- Customer B:
  - Searches for "office chairs" and buys one.
  - The AI recommends:
    - Ergonomic desk accessories (e.g., lumbar cushions, laptop stands).
    - A matching office desk with free shipping.

Benefits
- Improved Engagement: Customers spend more time on the platform exploring relevant products.
- Increased Sales: Personalized suggestions lead to higher conversion rates and cross-sells.
- Customer Loyalty: Users feel understood and valued, encouraging repeat purchases.

Other Applications of Personalization with Generative AI

1. Customer Support Responses:
   - AI chatbots provide personalized and context-aware assistance.
   - Example:
     - Customer: "Where is my order?"
     - AI Response: "Hi [Customer Name], your order of 'Wireless Earbuds Pro' is on the way and will be delivered by [Date]. Let me know if you'd like to track it further."
2. Content Personalization:
   - AI generates tailored content for users based on their interests.
   - Example:
     - A news platform uses AI to curate a personalized news feed for each subscriber, prioritizing topics they frequently read about (e.g., technology, sports).
3. Email Campaigns:
   - AI drafts highly personalized email content.
   - Example:

- Subject Line: "Just for You: 20% Off Your Favorite Running Gear!"
- Body: "Hi [Customer Name], based on your recent interest in running shoes, we thought you'd love our new collection. Shop now and enjoy an exclusive 20% discount!"

4. Streaming Platforms:
   - Recommending shows, movies, or songs tailored to user preferences.
   - Example:
     - Netflix uses generative AI to recommend shows based on a viewer's past watch history, ensuring a highly relevant and engaging experience.

Why Use Personalization?

1. Higher Conversion Rates: Personalized recommendations are more likely to resonate with users and lead to purchases.
2. Enhanced User Experience: Customers appreciate services that understand and anticipate their needs.
3. Increased Retention: Personalization fosters a sense of connection and loyalty to the platform.

Generative AI's ability to analyze user data and create personalized experiences revolutionizes customer interactions. Whether it's tailored product recommendations or individualized support responses, AI ensures that every user feels understood, valued, and engaged, driving business growth and customer satisfaction.

4. Simulations are Required:

Training AI Systems and Testing Scenarios

Simulations powered by Generative AI are indispensable when real-world testing is risky, expensive, or impractical. They create virtual environments that mimic reality, enabling organizations to train AI systems, test scenarios, or develop solutions without the constraints of physical environments.

Example Scenario: Training Autonomous Vehicles in a Simulated Environment

Problem: An autonomous vehicle (AV) company needs to train its AI system to navigate complex traffic scenarios, including dynamic events like sudden lane changes, unpredictable pedestrians, and adverse weather. Real-world testing is limited by:

- Risk: Testing in live traffic poses safety concerns.
- Cost: Setting up controlled environments is expensive and time-intensive.
- Edge Cases: Rare or dangerous scenarios (e.g., a child running onto the road) are difficult to replicate consistently.

Traditional Method

- The AV is tested in controlled environments such as closed tracks or monitored streets.
- Challenges:
    - Limited coverage of edge cases.
    - High setup and operational costs.
    - Lack of scalability to test all possible scenarios.

Generative AI Solution
- The company uses a generative AI-powered simulation platform to train its autonomous driving AI.

How It Works:
1. Creating the Simulation Environment:
   - Generative AI generates a virtual city with realistic roads, traffic signals, vehicles, pedestrians, and weather conditions.
   - The AI can modify environmental variables such as road types (urban, highway), traffic density, and visibility (fog, rain, night).
2. Introducing Dynamic Events:
   - The simulation includes edge cases, such as:
     - A pedestrian suddenly crossing the road.
     - Vehicles making unexpected lane changes.
     - Debris falling onto the highway.
   - Generative AI varies these events to test the AV system's adaptability.
3. Training the Autonomous Vehicle:
   - The AV system interacts with the simulated environment, collecting data to refine its decision-making algorithms.
   - Reinforcement learning trains the AI to optimize its actions (e.g., when to brake, accelerate, or steer) to maximize safety and efficiency.
4. Evaluating Performance:
   - The simulation measures key metrics such as:
     - Reaction time to unexpected events.
     - Accuracy of navigation in complex intersections.
     - Safety adherence under stress conditions.

Example in Action
- Scenario: Simulating a rainy urban environment with heavy pedestrian activity.
- Process:
    - Generative AI creates a bustling downtown street with realistic traffic and frequent jaywalking pedestrians.
    - The AV is tested on its ability to navigate without violating traffic rules or endangering pedestrians.
- Outcome:
    - The system learns to recognize pedestrian behavior patterns and anticipate their movements, improving its ability to stop in time under poor visibility conditions.

Benefits
- Risk-Free Training:
    - The AI system can be trained on rare or dangerous scenarios (e.g., vehicle skidding on black ice) without risking real-world harm.
- Cost-Effective:
    - Simulations reduce the need for expensive field tests and physical infrastructure.
- Scalability:
    - Hundreds of simulations can run simultaneously, covering diverse scenarios in less time.
- Improved AI Readiness:
    - The system is exposed to a broader range of situations, making it more robust and prepared for real-world deployment.

Other Applications of Simulations with Generative AI

1. Healthcare Simulations:
   ○ Example: Virtual patients are created to test new surgical techniques or train AI-powered diagnostic tools.
   ○ Scenario: Simulating a rare heart condition to train AI for early detection.
2. Military and Defense:
   ○ Example: Simulating battlefield scenarios for strategic planning or training autonomous drones.
   ○ Scenario: Testing drone navigation in a simulated hostile environment with unpredictable obstacles.
3. Robotics:
   ○ Example: Training warehouse robots in a virtual space to optimize picking, packing, and navigation.
   ○ Scenario: Simulating a high-demand period where robots must handle surges in activity.
4. Climate Modeling:
   ○ Example: Simulating weather patterns to test disaster response systems.
   ○ Scenario: Generative AI creates scenarios of hurricanes or floods to evaluate urban resilience strategies.

Why Use Simulations?

1. Safety:
   ○ Enables testing of high-risk scenarios without endangering lives or assets.
2. Cost-Efficiency:
   ○ Avoids expenses associated with real-world experiments and setups.
3. Comprehensive Testing:

    - Covers rare or edge cases that may not naturally occur in real-world tests.
4. Accelerated Development:
    - Speeds up training and testing cycles by enabling parallel simulations.

Generative AI-powered simulations are revolutionizing training and testing across industries. By creating realistic, dynamic environments, these simulations allow organizations to develop safer, more reliable systems while avoiding the risks and costs associated with real-world trials. In the case of autonomous vehicles, simulations provide the perfect blend of safety, scalability, and depth to train and test complex systems comprehensively.

6.5 When to Avoid Generative AI

Despite its power, there are scenarios where generative AI might not be suitable:

1. When Accuracy is Critical:
    - Generative AI might produce plausible-looking but factually incorrect content (e.g., generating misinformation in legal or medical documents).
2. When Data Quality is Insufficient:
    - Poor-quality or biased training data can lead to unreliable or biased outputs, which may harm decision-making or brand reputation.
3. When Ethical Concerns Arise:
    - Applications like deepfakes can be used

maliciously, leading to ethical and legal issues.
4. When Cost-Effectiveness is Questionable:
    o Developing and training generative models requires substantial computational resources. If simpler, rule-based approaches can achieve the same results, generative AI may not be worth the investment.
5. When Interpretability is Essential:
    o Generative AI models are often black-box systems, making it hard to explain how they arrived at a result, which might be problematic in industries like finance or healthcare.

Generative AI opens new possibilities for creating content, automating workflows, and simulating environments. While it has immense potential, decision-makers should carefully evaluate its suitability based on the context, ethical considerations, and resource constraints. By understanding its strengths and limitations, organizations can harness generative AI effectively while avoiding potential pitfalls.

7. EVALUATING AI POTENTIAL: QUESTIONS TO ASK BEFORE STARTING

Adopting Artificial Intelligence (AI) is a transformative step, but it's not one to take lightly. Before diving in, decision-makers need to evaluate whether AI aligns with their organizational needs, capabilities, and goals. This chapter provides a comprehensive framework to help leaders determine AI's relevance, ask critical questions, and assess its return on investment (ROI).

7.1 Determining AI's Relevance for Your Organization

AI is powerful, but it's not a universal solution. Not every business challenge requires AI, and understanding its relevance to your organization is the first step.

1. Identify the Core Problems AI Can Solve
    - Pinpoint the challenges your organization faces that AI could potentially address. Examples include:

- Inefficiencies: Are manual processes slowing down your operations?
- Lack of Insights: Do you struggle to extract actionable insights from large datasets?
- Customer Experience: Are customers expecting more personalized services that you can't currently deliver?
    - Example: A logistics company may identify that frequent delivery delays are caused by static route planning. AI could optimize routes using real-time traffic data.
2. Assess Data Availability and Quality
    - Data as the Foundation: AI models require large, high-quality datasets to function effectively.
    - Key questions to ask:
        - Do we have the necessary data?
        - Is the data clean, structured, and relevant to the problem we're solving?
        - Are there gaps in the data, and if so, how can we address them (e.g., by collecting new data)?
    - Example: A retailer with extensive customer transaction data could use AI for personalized recommendations, but a company lacking this data would struggle to deploy AI effectively.
3. Understand AI's Role in Your Industry
    - Research how AI is being used by competitors or other players in your industry. Common applications include:
        - Manufacturing: Predictive maintenance to prevent equipment failures.
        - Retail: Personalized product recommendations and dynamic pricing.
        - Healthcare: AI-assisted diagnosis and treatment planning.
    - Example: A hospital exploring AI could look at how other institutions use AI for triaging patients

or analyzing medical images.
4. Align AI with Strategic Goals
    - Ensure AI aligns with your organization's broader objectives, such as:
        - Increasing revenue.
        - Reducing operational costs.
        - Improving customer satisfaction.
    - Example: An e-commerce platform aiming to increase customer retention might implement AI-powered chatbots to provide personalized support and enhance user experiences.

7.2 Key Questions Decision-Makers Should Ask

Once you've determined AI's relevance, asking the right questions will help you evaluate its feasibility, risks, and alignment with organizational needs.

1. Strategic Questions
    - What is the specific problem we are trying to solve?
    - How will AI add measurable value to our business?
    - Is this a one-time use case, or will AI be a long-term part of our strategy?
    - Example: A food delivery company might ask whether AI can optimize routes in real-time and improve delivery speed by 20%.

2. Data-Related Questions
    - Do we have access to the necessary data to train and maintain AI systems?
    - Is the data diverse and unbiased, ensuring fair and accurate outcomes?

- Are there regulatory or privacy concerns with the data we intend to use?
- Example: A financial institution using AI for credit scoring must ensure customer data complies with GDPR or CCPA regulations.

3. Resource and Capability Questions
    - Do we have the technical expertise to implement and maintain AI systems? If not, should we:
        - Build in-house expertise?
        - Partner with external vendors or consultants?
    - What infrastructure (e.g., cloud platforms, computational resources) do we need to support AI?
    - Example: A small business considering AI-powered customer support might outsource its chatbot development to save costs.

4. Ethical and Risk Questions
    - How do we ensure AI operates transparently and without bias?
    - What safeguards will we put in place to address ethical concerns, such as job displacement or algorithmic bias?
    - How will AI impact employees, customers, and other stakeholders?
    - Example: A hiring platform using AI for candidate screening must ensure the algorithm doesn't favor or exclude certain demographics unfairly.

5. Success Measurement Questions
    - What does success look like for this AI project? What metrics will we use to measure it?
    - How will we monitor and continuously improve AI's performance over time?
    - Example: An AI-driven sales tool could measure success by tracking increased sales conversions and customer satisfaction ratings.

7.3 Understanding the ROI of AI

Evaluating the return on investment (ROI) of AI projects is essential to justify their implementation and ensure long-term sustainability.

1. Quantify Benefits
    - Tangible Benefits:
        - Cost savings through automation (e.g., reducing manual labor costs by automating repetitive tasks).
        - Revenue growth from personalized marketing or improved customer experiences.
        - Increased efficiency (e.g., faster production cycles in manufacturing).
    - Intangible Benefits:
        - Improved brand reputation as an innovator.
        - Enhanced employee satisfaction by automating mundane tasks.
    - Example: A customer service team might reduce call handling times by 30% using AI-powered chatbots, directly impacting operational efficiency.

2. Estimate Costs
    - Break down all associated costs, including:
        - Data collection, preparation, and storage.

- Infrastructure, such as cloud computing or on-premises servers.
- Development and integration of AI models.
- Ongoing maintenance, updates, and employee training.
  - Example: A retail company considering dynamic pricing with AI might calculate costs for acquiring transactional data, training models, and integrating with their e-commerce platform.

3. Balance Risks and Rewards
   - Consider potential risks, such as:
     - Failure due to poor data or unrealistic goals.
     - High initial costs without guaranteed short-term returns.
     - Reputational risks if AI makes incorrect or biased decisions.
   - Compare these risks against potential rewards to ensure informed decision-making.
   - Example: A financial institution might weigh the cost of building a fraud detection AI system against the potential savings from preventing fraudulent transactions.

4. Build a Business Case
   - Use ROI projections to create a compelling case for stakeholders. Highlight:
     - Measurable outcomes (e.g., increasing productivity by X%).
     - Cost savings over a defined period.
     - Strategic value to the organization.
   - Example: An AI-driven inventory management system might project reducing stock outs by 50%, increasing customer satisfaction and sales.

5. Plan for Long-Term ROI
   - Consider scalability and adaptability:

- Can the AI solution be expanded to other departments or use cases?
  - Will it adapt as business needs evolve?
  ○ Example: A logistics company might start with AI for route optimization but plan to expand it to predictive maintenance for its fleet.

Evaluating AI potential requires a balance of strategic thinking, resource assessment, and risk management. By determining AI's relevance, asking critical questions, and understanding ROI, decision-makers can ensure that AI becomes a strategic asset, driving measurable business outcomes while minimizing risks. This chapter provides the foundation for informed decision-making, setting the stage for successful AI adoption and long-term success.

8. BUILDING AN AI STRATEGY

Developing a robust AI strategy is essential for organizations aiming to leverage the transformative power of Artificial Intelligence. A well-crafted strategy ensures that AI initiatives align with your business goals, maximize ROI, and address potential challenges effectively. This chapter explores how to define clear goals and objectives, budget for AI projects, and align AI initiatives with your business vision.

8.1 Defining Goals and Objectives for AI

The foundation of any AI strategy lies in setting clear, measurable goals that align with your organization's overall mission. Without well-defined objectives, AI projects risk being aimless or failing to deliver meaningful outcomes.

Steps to Define AI Goals

1. Identify Business Challenges:
   - AI should address specific pain points or opportunities within your organization.
   - Examples:

- Customer Service: Reduce response times using AI-powered chatbots.
    - Operations: Automate repetitive tasks to improve efficiency.
    - Decision-Making: Use predictive analytics to improve forecasting accuracy.
  - Example: A manufacturing company identifies that frequent machine downtimes disrupt production. Its AI goal is to implement predictive maintenance to minimize downtime.
2. Set SMART Goals:
  - Ensure your goals are:
    - Specific: Focus on a single objective (e.g., "reduce order processing time by 20%").
    - Measurable: Define clear metrics to evaluate success.
    - Achievable: Base goals on realistic assessments of AI capabilities and resources.
    - Relevant: Align goals with business priorities.
    - Time-Bound: Set deadlines for achieving results.
  - Example: "Within six months, deploy an AI chatbot to reduce average customer service response times from 10 minutes to 2 minutes."
3. Prioritize Use Cases:
  - Evaluate potential AI applications based on:
    - Business impact: Will this significantly improve revenue, efficiency, or customer satisfaction?
    - Feasibility: Do we have the necessary data, expertise, and resources?
  - Example: A logistics company might prioritize AI for route optimization over predictive maintenance if delivery delays are a more pressing concern.
4. Involve Stakeholders:
  - Collaborate with key departments (e.g., IT, marketing, operations) to ensure alignment.
  - Get input from employees who will be directly

affected by AI adoption to gain buy-in and address concerns early.

8.2 How to Budget for AI Projects

AI initiatives require careful budgeting to ensure resources are allocated effectively and cost overruns are avoided. Budgeting for AI involves considering not just upfront costs but also long-term investments in infrastructure, talent, and maintenance.

Key Components of an AI Budget

1. Initial Investment:
   - Data Preparation:
     - Costs for collecting, cleaning, and structuring data.
     - Example: Hiring data engineers or purchasing third-party datasets.
   - Technology Stack:
     - Hardware: Servers, GPUs, or cloud services for AI computations.
     - Software: AI frameworks, development tools, and licenses.
     - Example: A retail company might budget for AWS cloud services to run its AI recommendation engine.

2. Talent and Expertise:
   - Costs for hiring or contracting:
     - Data scientists and AI engineers to develop models.
     - Domain experts to ensure AI solutions align with industry-specific needs.
     - Project managers to oversee implementation.
   - Example: A healthcare provider might hire an

AI consultant to integrate predictive analytics into patient care.
3. Development and Deployment:
   - Budget for:
     - Model training: Computational resources to train AI models.
     - Integration: Connecting AI tools with existing systems (e.g., ERP, CRM).
     - Pilot projects: Testing AI solutions on a smaller scale before full rollout.
   - Example: A logistics firm might allocate funds for testing AI-powered delivery route optimization in one region before scaling.
4. Ongoing Costs:
   - Maintenance:
     - Updating models as data evolves or business needs change.
     - Monitoring performance to ensure AI continues to meet objectives.
   - Training:
     - Continuous employee training to use AI tools effectively.
     - Example: An e-commerce company might hold regular training sessions for its marketing team on using AI analytics dashboards.
   - Scaling:
     - Expanding AI solutions to other departments or geographies.
5. Estimating ROI
   - Weigh expected benefits against costs to evaluate the feasibility of AI investments.
   - Example: A company projects a 20% reduction in operational costs through AI automation, outweighing the initial investment over two years.

8.3 Aligning AI with Your Business Vision

AI should not exist in isolation—it must integrate seamlessly into your organization's broader strategy and vision. This ensures that AI initiatives are impactful, sustainable, and aligned with long-term goals.

Steps to Align AI with Business Vision

1. Understand the Big Picture:
    - Revisit your organization's mission, vision, and strategic goals.
    - Ask:
        - How can AI help us achieve these goals?
        - What competitive advantages can AI provide?
    - Example: A renewable energy company with a mission to reduce carbon emissions might use AI to optimize energy distribution, ensuring minimal waste and maximum efficiency.
2. Create a Roadmap:
    - Develop a phased approach to implementing AI:
        - Phase 1: Pilot projects to test feasibility (e.g., using AI for demand forecasting in one region).
        - Phase 2: Full-scale implementation (e.g., rolling out AI-driven forecasting nationwide).
        - Phase 3: Expansion into new use cases or departments.
3. Build Cross-Functional Collaboration:
    - AI initiatives require input from various departments:
        - IT ensures technical feasibility.
        - Operations define process needs.
        - Marketing and sales use insights to tailor customer strategies.
    - Example: In a retail chain, AI for personalized

recommendations requires collaboration between marketing (for customer insights) and IT (for integration into e-commerce platforms).
4. Communicate AI's Role Clearly:
    - Ensure that employees and stakeholders understand:
        - Why AI is being adopted.
        - How it will benefit the organization and individuals.
    - Example: A logistics firm explains to drivers how AI-powered route optimization tools will reduce their workload and improve delivery times.
5. Adapt to Change:
    - Continuously monitor industry trends and adapt your AI strategy accordingly.
    - Example: A media company may initially use AI for content recommendation but later expand into generative AI for creating personalized video summaries as customer preferences evolve.

Building an AI strategy requires clear goals, realistic budgeting, and alignment with your organization's vision. By defining specific objectives, carefully planning resources, and integrating AI into your broader strategy, you can ensure its successful adoption and maximize its impact. This chapter equips you with the tools to make AI a cornerstone of your organization's success.

9. CHOOSING THE RIGHT AI TEAM

The success of any AI initiative hinges on assembling the right team to bring your vision to life. Building or collaborating with an AI team requires a balance of technical expertise, industry knowledge, and strategic alignment. This chapter explores who you need on your team, whether to work with AI vendors or build in-house, and how to foster effective collaboration between technical and non-technical stakeholders.

9.1 Who You Need: Data Scientists, Engineers & Domain Experts

AI projects require a diverse team with complementary skills. Here's a breakdown of key roles and why they're critical:

1. Data Scientists

- Role: Data scientists are the architects of AI models. They analyze data, select algorithms, and train models to solve specific problems.
- Responsibilities:
  - Data cleaning and preparation.
  - Developing and testing machine learning models.

- o   Interpreting results and refining models for accuracy.
- Skills: Proficiency in programming (e.g., Python, R), machine learning frameworks (e.g., TensorFlow, PyTorch), and data visualization.
- Why They're Important: Without data scientists, AI systems lack the core logic needed to deliver results.

2. AI/ML Engineers

- Role: Engineers take the models developed by data scientists and deploy them into production systems.
- Responsibilities:
  - o   Building scalable AI pipelines and APIs.
  - o   Integrating AI solutions into existing software.
  - o   Monitoring and maintaining deployed models.
- Skills: Expertise in software engineering, cloud platforms (e.g., AWS, Azure), and DevOps tools.
- Why They're Important: Engineers ensure AI solutions are functional, scalable, and accessible to end users.

3. Domain Experts

- Role: These professionals provide industry-specific knowledge that guides AI development.
- Responsibilities:
  - o   Ensuring the AI solution aligns with business needs.
  - o   Identifying key data features and metrics.
  - o   Validating AI outputs for accuracy and relevance.
- Skills: Deep understanding of the industry and the specific problem AI aims to solve.
- Why They're Important: AI needs context to be effective. Domain experts ensure solutions address real-world challenges.

4. Project Managers

- Role: Project managers coordinate the AI team, keeping projects on track and aligned with business goals.
- Responsibilities:

- - Managing timelines, budgets, and milestones.
  - Facilitating communication between technical and non-technical teams.
  - Ensuring deliverables meet business requirements.
- Why They're Important: They bridge the gap between leadership and the technical team, ensuring clarity and focus.

5. UX Designers (Optional)

- Role: User experience designers ensure that AI tools are user-friendly and accessible.
- Responsibilities:
  - Designing intuitive interfaces for AI-driven applications.
  - Conducting user testing and feedback sessions.
- Why They're Important: A well-designed AI tool improves adoption rates and end-user satisfaction.

9.2 Working with AI Vendors vs. Building In-House

Deciding whether to partner with AI vendors or build your own in-house team depends on your organization's needs, resources, and goals.

1. Working with AI Vendors

- Benefits:
  - Speed: Vendors often have ready-made solutions that can be quickly customized.
  - Expertise: Access to highly skilled teams without hiring full-time employees.
  - Cost Efficiency: Ideal for companies with limited budgets or short-term projects.
- Challenges:
  - Limited Customization: Off-the-shelf solutions may not fully align with unique business needs.

- - Dependence: Long-term reliance on external vendors can limit flexibility.
- Best For:
  - Organizations new to AI that need quick wins.
  - Short-term projects or pilot implementations.
  - Companies with limited technical expertise.

2. Building an In-House AI Team

- Benefits:
  - Full Control: Tailor AI solutions to align precisely with business goals.
  - Long-Term Value: Develop internal capabilities for sustained innovation.
  - Data Security: Greater control over sensitive data.
- Challenges:
  - High Costs: Hiring skilled talent and investing in infrastructure can be expensive.
  - Time-Intensive: Building a team and developing solutions takes time.
- Best For:
  - Organizations with significant, long-term AI ambitions.
  - Companies with sufficient resources and a commitment to developing internal expertise.

3. A Hybrid Approach

- Many companies use a hybrid model, combining external expertise with in-house talent:
  - Vendors manage initial development, while in-house teams handle maintenance and customization.
  - Example: A healthcare provider partners with an AI vendor to build a diagnostic model but hires in-house data scientists to continuously refine it.

9.3 Tips for Effective Collaboration

Between Technical and Non-Technical Teams

AI projects often fail not because of technology, but due to poor communication and misalignment between teams. Here's how to foster collaboration:

1. Speak a Common Language

- Encourage technical teams to explain AI concepts in simple, non-technical terms.
- Educate non-technical stakeholders on basic AI principles, so they can understand possibilities and limitations.
- Example: A data scientist explains predictive analytics as "forecasting future trends based on patterns in historical data."

2. Define Clear Objectives

- Align all teams on what the AI project aims to achieve.
- Break goals into measurable milestones that everyone understands.
- Example: Instead of saying "Improve efficiency," define success as "Reduce customer service response times by 30% within six months."

3. Foster Regular Communication

- Schedule regular meetings between technical and non-technical teams to:
    - Share updates.
    - Address challenges early.
    - Align progress with business goals.
- Use collaborative tools like project management software (e.g., Jira, Trello) to keep everyone informed.

4. Involve End Users Early

- Engage end users (e.g., customer service agents, sales teams) during the design and testing phases.

- Collect feedback to ensure the AI solution meets practical needs and is user-friendly.
- Example: A retail company includes store managers in testing an AI inventory system to ensure it aligns with on-the-ground realities.

5. Create a Feedback Loop

- Encourage feedback from both technical and non-technical stakeholders to continuously refine the AI system.
- Use this input to address blind spots, improve functionality, and ensure alignment with business needs.

Building the right AI team and fostering collaboration between technical and non-technical teams are critical for the success of your AI initiatives. By carefully selecting the right talent, deciding whether to work with vendors or build in-house, and prioritizing clear communication and alignment, you can ensure your AI projects deliver real value to your organization.

10. THE ETHICAL AND REGULATORY LANDSCAPE

As Artificial Intelligence (AI) becomes increasingly integrated into everyday life, its ethical and regulatory implications demand serious attention. Organizations must address ethical considerations, adhere to data privacy regulations, and proactively manage bias to ensure AI is used responsibly and equitably. This chapter explores the principles of AI ethics, relevant regulations, and strategies for mitigating bias and promoting fairness.

10.1 Understanding AI Ethics and Responsible AI

AI ethics refers to the principles and practices that ensure AI technologies are developed and deployed in ways that are fair, transparent, and beneficial to society. Responsible AI goes beyond compliance to proactively address potential risks and challenges.

Core Principles of AI Ethics

1. Transparency:
- AI systems should operate in ways that are understandable to users and stakeholders.
- Decision-making processes must be explainable, especially in critical applications like healthcare and finance.
- Example: A bank using AI for loan approvals should explain how the algorithm evaluates creditworthiness.

2. Accountability:
- Organizations must take responsibility for the outcomes of their AI systems.
- Clear ownership ensures ethical breaches or unintended consequences are addressed promptly.
- Example: A hiring platform should be accountable for any biases in its AI-powered recruitment tool.

3. Privacy:
- AI systems must safeguard personal data and comply with regulations like GDPR (General Data Protection Regulation) and CCPA (California Consumer Privacy Act).
- Data should only be collected and used with clear consent and for legitimate purposes.
- Example: An AI-driven healthcare app must anonymize patient data to protect individual identities.

4. Equity:
- AI should not discriminate against individuals based on factors like race, gender, age, or socioeconomic status.
- Ethical AI systems promote inclusivity and fairness.
- Example: A facial recognition system should perform equally well across diverse demographic groups.

5. Benefits:
    o   AI should be designed to improve human well-being and avoid harm.
    o   It should align with societal values and enhance quality of life.
    o   Example: Autonomous vehicles should prioritize passenger safety and pedestrian welfare.

Regulations Around AI and Data Privacy

Governments and international organizations are introducing regulations to address ethical concerns and protect individuals' rights. Decision-makers must stay informed about these laws and integrate compliance into their AI strategies.

1. *General Data Protection Regulation (GDPR)* (EU):
    o   Focuses on data privacy and security.
    o   Key requirements:
        ▪   Consent for data collection.
        ▪   The right to access, correct, or delete personal data.
        ▪   Strict penalties for breaches.
    o   Example: A European e-commerce platform using AI for personalized recommendations must allow customers to opt out of data collection.
2. *California Consumer Privacy Act (CCPA)* (USA):
    o   Empowers consumers to control their personal data.
    o   Requirements:
        ▪   Disclosure of data collection practices.
        ▪   The right to opt out of data sharing.
    o   Example: A U.S.-based retailer must provide customers with a clear option to disable AI-based tracking.
3. AI-Specific Policies:
    o   Countries are introducing AI-focused frameworks:
        ▪   EU's AI Act: Categorizes AI applications based on risk levels, requiring stricter compliance for

high-risk systems like biometric identification.
- China's AI Guidelines: Emphasize algorithm transparency and national security.

10.2 Managing Bias and Ensuring Fairness

AI systems can inadvertently perpetuate or amplify bias, leading to unfair outcomes. Managing bias is not just an ethical necessity but also a legal and reputational imperative.

What Causes Bias in AI?

1. Biased Training Data:
   - AI learns from historical data, which may reflect societal biases.
   - Example: A hiring algorithm trained on past recruitment data may favor male candidates if the company historically hired more men.
2. Algorithmic Design:
   - The way algorithms are programmed can introduce biases.
   - Example: A credit scoring system might assign higher weight to variables that disproportionately disadvantage specific groups.
3. Underrepresentation:
   - Insufficient data from certain demographics can lead to poor performance for those groups.
   - Example: Facial recognition systems that perform poorly on darker skin tones due to limited training data.

Strategies to Mitigate Bias

1. Diverse Training Data:
   - Ensure datasets are representative of all relevant demographics.

- Regularly audit data for imbalances or gaps.
- Example: A medical diagnosis AI should include data from patients of varying ages, genders, and ethnicities.

2. Bias Audits:
- Conduct regular audits of AI models to identify and address biases.
- Use tools like IBM's AI Fairness 360 or Google's What-If Tool for bias detection.
- Example: A loan approval AI can be audited to ensure it doesn't disproportionately reject applications from minority groups.

3. Explainable AI (XAI):
- Develop models that provide clear, interpretable insights into how decisions are made.
- Example: An HR tool using AI for candidate screening should explain why a candidate was rejected or recommended.

4. Human Oversight:
- Combine AI decisions with human judgment, particularly in high-stakes scenarios.
- Example: A bank using AI for fraud detection should have human analysts review flagged cases to avoid false positives.

5. Ethical Review Boards:
- Establish internal committees to oversee AI projects and ensure they meet ethical standards.
- Example: A healthcare organization can create an ethics board to review AI systems used for patient care.

Ensuring Fairness

1. Preemptive Testing:
- Test AI models on diverse scenarios before deployment to identify unfair outcomes.
- Example: A university testing an AI admissions

tool should simulate its performance across different applicant demographics.
2. Feedback Loops:
   o Allow users to report unfair or inaccurate AI outcomes.
   o Use this feedback to improve the system.
   o Example: A social media platform using AI for content moderation can provide a "dispute" option for flagged posts.
3. Continuous Monitoring:
   o Monitor AI systems regularly to detect and correct biases as data evolves.
   o Example: A retail company uses AI to adjust dynamic pricing but monitors to ensure fairness across customer segments.

Addressing the ethical and regulatory landscape is critical for successful and responsible AI deployment. By prioritizing transparency, accountability, and fairness, organizations can build trust and comply with evolving regulations. Managing bias and ensuring fairness are ongoing responsibilities that require proactive strategies, robust testing, and continuous monitoring. Adopting ethical AI practices is not just about compliance—it's about creating technology that serves and uplifts society

11. THE FUTURE OF AI IN BUSINESS

As Artificial Intelligence (AI) evolves, its impact on business becomes more profound. From emerging trends to transformative industry changes, AI is reshaping the way organizations operate, innovate, and compete. Understanding these developments and preparing for an AI-driven future is crucial for decision-makers.

11.1 Upcoming Trends in AI

The future of AI will be defined by technological advancements and new use cases that push the boundaries of what's possible. Here are the most significant trends to watch:

1. Generative AI Becomes Mainstream

- What It Is: Generative AI, such as GPT and DALL-E, creates new content, including text, images, videos, and even software code.
- Applications:
  - Content Creation: Automating marketing copy, video editing, and product design.
  - Product Development: Generating new prototypes or 3D models for manufacturing.
  - Customer Engagement: Personalizing interactions

through AI-generated responses.
- Future Outlook: Generative AI tools will become more accessible and customizable, enabling businesses to scale creative tasks and reduce costs.

2. AI Augmenting Human Decision-Making

- What It Is: AI increasingly acts as a co-pilot, assisting humans in complex decision-making.
- Applications:
  o Finance: AI models predict market trends and guide investment strategies.
  o Healthcare: AI supports doctors by suggesting diagnoses or treatment plans based on data.
  o Operations: AI helps managers optimize supply chains and resource allocation.
- Future Outlook: Decision-support systems will integrate seamlessly into workflows, blending human intuition with AI-driven insights.

3. AI-Driven Automation Across More Sectors

- What It Is: AI-powered robots and software automate not just repetitive tasks but also decision-intensive processes.
- Applications:
  o Manufacturing: Robots perform complex assembly tasks.
  o Customer Support: AI chatbots handle customer inquiries with human-like efficiency.
  o Legal and Compliance: AI automates document review and regulatory checks.
- Future Outlook: Automation will expand into knowledge-intensive fields, like legal analysis and scientific research.

4. Democratization of AI Tools

- What It Is: AI platforms are becoming more user-friendly, enabling non-technical users to leverage AI without extensive coding knowledge.

- Applications:
  - No-Code/Low-Code Platforms: Tools like Microsoft Power Automate allow users to build AI workflows with minimal effort.
  - Custom AI Models: Businesses will be able to train AI on their own data using plug-and-play solutions.
- Future Outlook: Democratization will empower small and medium-sized businesses (SMBs) to adopt AI, leveling the playing field.

5. AI Ethics and Regulation Take Center Stage

- What It Is: As AI adoption grows, concerns around ethics, transparency, and fairness will drive stricter regulations.
- Future Outlook: Companies will need to prioritize ethical AI practices to comply with evolving regulations and maintain customer trust.

11.2 How AI Will Continue to Change Industries

AI is not just automating processes—it's fundamentally transforming the way industries operate, innovate, and deliver value. Here's how AI will impact key sectors:

1. Healthcare

- Current Impact:
  - AI assists in diagnosing diseases from medical images.
  - Predictive analytics identifies patients at risk of complications.
- Future Impact:
  - Personalized Medicine: AI will analyze genetic data to tailor treatments to individual patients.
  - Virtual Health Assistants: AI-powered apps will provide round-the-clock healthcare advice, reducing strain on medical staff.

- Drug Discovery: AI will accelerate the development of new drugs by identifying promising compounds faster.

2. Retail and E-Commerce
    - Current Impact:
        - Personalized product recommendations.
        - Dynamic pricing strategies based on customer behavior and demand.
    - Future Impact:
        - Hyper-Personalization: AI will create tailored shopping experiences for individual customers in real-time.
        - Autonomous Stores: AI-enabled checkout-free stores will become more common, enhancing convenience.
        - Visual Search: Customers will use images to search for and purchase products.

3. Manufacturing
    - Current Impact:
        - Predictive maintenance reduces equipment downtime.
        - AI optimizes production schedules.
    - Future Impact:
        - Smart Factories: Fully automated factories powered by AI and IoT will adapt to changing demand in real time.
        - Sustainable Production: AI will minimize waste and energy consumption in manufacturing processes.

4. Finance
    - Current Impact:
        - Fraud detection through anomaly detection algorithms.
        - Credit scoring using machine learning models.
    - Future Impact:

- o   Real-Time Risk Assessment: AI will continuously monitor market conditions and adjust investment strategies.
- o   Automated Financial Advising: AI advisors will provide personalized investment recommendations.

5. Transportation and Logistics
- Current Impact:
    - o   AI optimizes delivery routes using real-time traffic data.
    - o   Autonomous vehicles are being tested for freight transport.
- Future Impact:
    - o   End-to-End Automation: Entire supply chains will operate autonomously, from warehouse robots to last-mile delivery drones.
    - o   Sustainable Logistics: AI will optimize transportation routes to reduce carbon emissions.

11.3 Preparing for an AI-Driven Future

To thrive in an AI-dominated landscape, organizations must adopt proactive strategies. Here's how to prepare for the changes ahead:

1. Invest in AI Literacy
- Why It Matters: AI success depends on an informed workforce that understands how to work alongside intelligent systems.
- How to Do It:
    - o   Conduct AI training programs for employees at all levels.
    - o   Provide non-technical teams with basic AI knowledge to improve collaboration with technical experts.

- o   Encourage continuous learning to keep up with evolving AI trends.

2. Build an AI-Ready Culture

- Why It Matters: Organizational resistance can derail AI projects, even when the technology is sound.
- How to Do It:
  - o   Foster a culture of innovation by rewarding experimentation.
  - o   Address fears of job displacement by focusing on AI as a tool for augmentation, not replacement.
  - o   Encourage cross-functional collaboration to align AI initiatives with business goals.

3. Upgrade Infrastructure

- Why It Matters: AI requires robust computing power, storage, and data management capabilities.
- How to Do It:
  - o   Invest in scalable cloud platforms to handle AI workloads.
  - o   Implement data pipelines for efficient collection, storage, and analysis.
  - o   Ensure cybersecurity measures are in place to protect sensitive data.

4. Focus on Ethical AI

- Why It Matters: Trust is crucial for long-term success, and unethical AI practices can lead to reputational damage and regulatory penalties.
- How to Do It:
  - o   Conduct regular audits to detect bias and ensure fairness.
  - o   Implement explainable AI models to improve transparency.
  - o   Stay compliant with emerging AI regulations.

5. Experiment with Scalable Pilot Projects

- Why It Matters: Starting small reduces risk and provides valuable insights for scaling AI initiatives.
- How to Do It:
    - Launch pilot projects in high-impact areas, such as customer support or logistics.
    - Measure success through clear metrics like cost savings, efficiency improvements, or customer satisfaction.
    - Use pilot results to refine your approach before full-scale implementation.

6. Develop Long-Term Partnerships

- Why It Matters: Collaborating with AI vendors, research institutions, and tech partners can accelerate AI adoption.
- How to Do It:
    - Partner with universities to access cutting-edge research.
    - Work with cloud providers for scalable AI infrastructure.
    - Collaborate with industry peers to share insights and best practices.

The future of AI in business is one of transformation, innovation, and opportunity. By staying ahead of trends, embracing AI-driven changes in industries, and preparing strategically, organizations can unlock AI's full potential. This chapter provides the roadmap for decision-makers to lead in an AI-dominated future, ensuring they are not only prepared but positioned to thrive.

12. GLOSSARY OF KEY AI TERMS

Understanding Artificial Intelligence (AI) requires familiarity with its foundational terms and concepts. This glossary provides simplified definitions for the most essential AI-related terms, enabling decision-makers to grasp the core ideas and technologies shaping the field.

12.1 Simplified Definitions of AI Concepts and Terms

A

1. Artificial Intelligence (AI):
   The simulation of human intelligence in machines, enabling them to perform tasks like problem-solving, learning, and decision-making.
2. Algorithm:
   A set of step-by-step instructions a computer follows to solve a problem or perform a task.
3. Artificial Neural Network (ANN):
   A computing system inspired by the structure of the human brain, consisting of layers of interconnected nodes (neurons) that process information.
4. Autonomous Systems:

Machines or software that operate independently without human intervention, such as self-driving cars or drones.

B

5. Bias in AI:
Systematic errors in AI outputs caused by biased training data or flawed algorithms, leading to unfair or inaccurate results.
6. Big Data:
Extremely large datasets that require specialized tools and techniques, like AI, to analyze and extract insights.
7. Black Box Model:
An AI system whose inner workings are not easily understood, making it difficult to explain how decisions are made.
8. Bayesian Network:
A probabilistic model that represents variables and their relationships to predict outcomes or make decisions under uncertainty.

C

9. Chatbot:
An AI-powered virtual assistant that can simulate human conversation to answer questions, provide information, or assist with tasks.
10. Cloud Computing:
Delivering computing services like storage, processing, and AI tools over the internet, enabling scalability and cost efficiency.
11. Computer Vision:
A field of AI focused on enabling machines to interpret and understand visual information from images or videos.
12. Clustering:

An unsupervised learning technique that groups similar data points together based on shared characteristics.

D

13.	Data Cleaning:
The process of removing or correcting errors and inconsistencies in datasets to ensure AI models produce accurate results.
14.	Data Mining:
Extracting useful patterns, trends, and insights from large datasets using AI and statistical techniques.
15.	Deep Learning:
A subset of machine learning that uses neural networks with many layers (deep networks) to analyze and learn from large amounts of data.
16.	Dimensionality Reduction:
A technique used to simplify datasets by reducing the number of variables while retaining important information.

E

17.	Explainable AI (XAI):
AI systems designed to provide clear, understandable explanations for how decisions are made.
18.	Edge Computing:
Processing data near its source (e.g., IoT devices) rather than relying on a central cloud server, improving speed and efficiency.
19.	Ethical AI:
The development and deployment of AI systems that are fair, transparent, and beneficial to society.

F

20.	Feature Engineering:

The process of selecting, transforming, and creating data features to improve the performance of AI models.

21. Federated Learning:
A machine learning approach where data remains on local devices, and only the model updates are shared, enhancing privacy.

22. Fine-Tuning:
Adjusting a pre-trained AI model to specialize in a specific task by training it on additional data.

G

23. Generative AI:
AI models, such as GANs or transformers, that can create new content like text, images, or music.

24. Generative Adversarial Networks (GANs):
A type of AI model that uses two networks (a generator and a discriminator) to create realistic synthetic data, such as lifelike images.

25. Gradient Descent:
An optimization algorithm used to train AI models by minimizing errors in predictions.

H

26. Hyperparameters:
Settings or configurations (e.g., learning rate, number of layers) that control how an AI model learns during training.

27. Human-in-the-Loop (HITL):
A system where humans actively intervene or oversee AI processes to improve accuracy and fairness.

28. Heuristics:
Simple rules or strategies that AI systems use to make decisions or solve problems efficiently.

I

29. Internet of Things (IoT):
A network of interconnected devices that collect and share data, often powered by AI for real-time analytics.

30. Image Recognition:
An application of computer vision where AI identifies and classifies objects or features in images.

31. Inference:
The process where an AI model uses learned knowledge to make predictions or decisions on new data.

L

32. Labeling:
Annotating data with meaningful tags (e.g., "cat" or "dog" for an image) for supervised machine learning training.

33. Large Language Models (LLMs):
AI models, like GPT, designed to understand and generate human-like text by processing vast amounts of language data.

34. Linear Regression:
A statistical method used in machine learning to predict a target value based on input variables.

35. Logistic Regression:
A machine learning algorithm used for binary classification tasks, such as spam detection.

M

36. Machine Learning (ML):
A subset of AI where machines learn from data and improve over time without explicit programming.

37. Model Training:
The process of teaching an AI model to recognize patterns and make predictions by exposing it to data.

38. Multimodal AI:
AI systems capable of processing and integrating multiple types of data (e.g., text, images, and audio) simultaneously.

N

39. Natural Language Processing (NLP):
A branch of AI that enables machines to understand, interpret, and generate human language.
40. Neural Network:
A computational model inspired by the human brain, consisting of layers of interconnected nodes for processing data.
41. Normalization:
Scaling data to a consistent range to improve the performance and stability of AI models.

P

42. Predictive Analytics:
Using AI and statistical models to predict future trends or outcomes based on historical data.
43. Pre-trained Models:
AI models trained on large datasets that can be fine-tuned for specific tasks, reducing the need for extensive training.
44. Precision and Recall:
Metrics used to evaluate the performance of AI models, focusing on accuracy (precision) and the ability to detect all relevant instances (recall).

R

45. Reinforcement Learning (RL):
An AI learning approach where agents learn by interacting with their environment and receiving rewards or penalties.

46. Regression:
A machine learning technique used to predict continuous values, such as sales revenue or temperature.

47. ResNet:
A type of deep learning model designed to address challenges in training very deep neural networks.

T

48. Training Data: The dataset used to teach an AI model during its development. The model learns patterns, relationships, and trends from this data to make predictions or decisions on new data.

49. Transfer Learning: A machine learning technique where a pre-trained model is adapted to a new, related task. This approach saves time and computational resources by leveraging existing knowledge.

50. Turing Test: A test proposed by Alan Turing to evaluate a machine's ability to exhibit intelligent behavior indistinguishable from a human. If a human evaluator cannot reliably differentiate between responses from a machine and a human, the machine passes the test.

51. TensorFlow: An open-source machine learning framework developed by Google, widely used for building and deploying AI models, especially deep learning applications.

52. Tokenization: The process of breaking down text into smaller units (tokens), such as words or subwords, for analysis in natural language processing (NLP) tasks.

U

53. Unsupervised Learning: A type of machine learning where the model is trained on unlabeled data, aiming to identify hidden patterns, structures, or relationships within the dataset. Examples include clustering and dimensionality reduction.

54. User Experience (UX) in AI: Designing AI systems to be user-friendly and intuitive, ensuring that end-users can effectively interact with and benefit from AI tools.

55. Universal Approximation Theorem: A concept in neural networks stating that a feedforward network with a single hidden layer can approximate any continuous function, given sufficient neurons.

V

59. Validation Data: A subset of data used during the training process to evaluate the performance of the AI model and fine-tune its parameters. It helps prevent overfitting.

60. Variance: In machine learning, variance refers to a model's sensitivity to fluctuations in the training dataset. High variance can lead to overfitting, where the model performs well on training data but poorly on new data.

61. Visual Recognition: A subset of computer vision where AI models are trained to identify and classify objects, scenes, or activities in images or videos.

W

62. Weak AI: Also known as narrow AI, this refers to AI systems designed to perform specific tasks or solve particular problems. Unlike strong AI, weak AI does not possess general intelligence.

63. Weight (in Neural Networks): A parameter in a neural network that adjusts the strength of the connection between nodes (neurons). Weights are updated during training to improve the model's predictions.

64. Word Embedding: A technique used in NLP to represent words as dense vectors in a multi-dimensional space, capturing semantic relationships and similarities between words.

X

65. Explainable AI (XAI): AI systems designed to provide transparent and understandable explanations for their decisions, ensuring trust and accountability.

66. XML (Extensible Markup Language): A data format used for structuring and storing data in a machine-readable way, often employed in AI for data exchange and configuration.

Y

67. YOLO (You Only Look Once): A popular real-time object detection algorithm that processes images in a single step, identifying multiple objects with high accuracy and speed.

68. Yield Prediction (Agriculture): An

application of AI in farming that predicts crop yields based on factors like weather, soil conditions, and historical data.

Z

69. Zero-Shot Learning: A machine learning technique where a model can recognize and categorize objects or tasks it has never seen during training, using contextual knowledge or related examples.

70. Z-Score Normalization: A statistical method used to standardize data by subtracting the mean and dividing by the standard deviation, ensuring consistency across features.

13. AI TOOLS AND PLATFORMS FOR BEGINNERS

The rise of user-friendly AI tools and platforms has made Artificial Intelligence more accessible than ever, even for individuals and organizations without deep technical expertise. Whether you're a business leader, a beginner in AI, or part of a small team, these tools can help you harness the power of AI with minimal coding or specialized knowledge.

13.1 Overview of User-Friendly AI Tools

AI platforms have evolved to simplify the complex processes of data analysis, model creation, and deployment. These tools are designed to enable beginners and non-technical users to implement AI solutions effectively.

1. AutoML (Automated Machine Learning)
- What It Is:
  - AutoML automates the end-to-end process of

applying machine learning, from preprocessing data to selecting the best model.
- Ideal for beginners who need insights but lack expertise in ML.
- Key Features:
  - Data preprocessing (e.g., cleaning, feature engineering).
  - Model selection and hyperparameter tuning.
  - Performance evaluation and easy deployment.
- Popular Tools:
  - **Google Cloud AutoML**: Offers a suite of tools for image recognition, natural language processing, and structured data analysis. Users simply upload datasets, and the platform automates the rest.
  - **Microsoft Azure AutoML**: A user-friendly solution for building and deploying predictive models without coding.
  - **AWS** is a powerful and versatile platform for AI beginners, offering user-friendly tools like SageMaker Canvas, Rekognition, Polly, and Lex to simplify complex AI tasks. Its low-code and no-code platforms enable businesses to implement AI solutions quickly and effectively, making it a go-to choice for organizations starting their AI journey.
- Use Case Example:
  - A retail company uses AutoML to predict customer churn by analyzing historical sales and behavior data

2. DataRobot
- What It Is:
  - DataRobot is an enterprise AI platform that automates the entire data science workflow.
- Key Features:
  - Automated model building and comparison.
  - Insights and interpretability tools for understanding results.

- o Deployment options for integrating models into applications.
- Why It's Beginner-Friendly:
  - o Intuitive dashboards make it easy for business users to interact with models.
- Use Case Example:
  - o A financial institution uses DataRobot to predict loan defaults by training models on customer demographics and repayment history.

3. H2O.ai

- What It Is:
  - o An open-source AutoML platform for building machine learning models.
- Key Features:
  - o Supports various data formats and integrates with popular tools like Python and R.
  - o Offers H2O Driverless AI for automated machine learning.
- Use Case Example:
  - o A healthcare provider uses H2O.ai to analyze patient records and predict hospital readmission risks.

4. IBM Watson Studio

- What It Is:
  - o A cloud-based AI platform offering a suite of tools for beginners and advanced users.
- Key Features:
  - o Pre-built AI solutions for industries like healthcare, finance, and retail.
  - o No-code tools for exploring data and building models.
- Why It's Beginner-Friendly:
  - o Drag-and-drop interfaces simplify AI workflows.
- Use Case Example:
  - o A logistics company uses Watson Studio to optimize delivery routes using AI-driven predictive analytics.

5. Teachable Machine (Google)
   - What It Is:
     - A beginner-friendly tool for creating AI models using a web browser, without coding.
   - Key Features:
     - Enables users to train models for image, sound, and pose recognition.
     - Simplifies AI by using drag-and-drop features.
   - Use Case Example:
     - A teacher creates a Teachable Machine model to recognize students' gestures for interactive classroom activities.

13.2 Low-Code and No-Code AI Platforms

Low-code and no-code platforms are democratizing AI by empowering individuals with little or no programming knowledge to build and deploy AI applications.

1. What Are Low-Code and No-Code Platforms?
   - Low-Code Platforms:
     - Allow users to build AI applications with minimal coding, using pre-built components and visual interfaces.
     - Ideal for users with basic technical skills who want more customization.
   - No-Code Platforms:
     - Require no programming skills and use drag-and-drop tools for creating AI workflows.
     - Perfect for non-technical users seeking quick solutions.

2. Popular Low-Code and No-Code AI Platforms
   1. Microsoft Power Platform (Power Automate and Power BI):

- What It Does:
    - Power Automate: Automates workflows using AI.
    - Power BI: Generates AI-powered data visualizations and insights.
- Why It's Beginner-Friendly:
    - Intuitive interface for integrating AI into business processes.
- Use Case Example:
    - A sales team uses Power BI to create dashboards showing predictive sales trends.

2. MonkeyLearn:
- What It Does:
    - A no-code platform for text analysis, such as sentiment analysis, keyword extraction, and classification.
- Why It's Beginner-Friendly:
    - Simple drag-and-drop tools for building AI-powered text workflows.
- Use Case Example:
    - A customer support team uses MonkeyLearn to analyze feedback and classify tickets by urgency.

3. BigML:
- What It Does:
    - Offers no-code machine learning tools for creating models and visualizing data.
- Why It's Beginner-Friendly:
    - Focuses on simplicity and clarity in workflows.
- Use Case Example:
    - An educator uses BigML to predict student performance based on attendance and grades.

4. Lobe:
- What It Does:
    - A no-code AI platform for building and training

custom machine learning models.
- Why It's Beginner-Friendly:
  - Intuitive interface designed for complete beginners.
- Use Case Example:
  - A photographer uses Lobe to classify images into categories automatically.

5. RunwayML:
- What It Does:
  - Simplifies the use of AI in creative industries like video editing, image generation, and sound design.
- Why It's Beginner-Friendly:
  - Accessible tools tailored for non-technical creative professionals.
- Use Case Example:
  - A video producer uses RunwayML to automate editing tasks like background removal.

13.3 Advantages of Low-Code and No-Code Platforms

1. Accessibility:
   - Removes barriers to AI adoption for non-technical users.
   - Encourages experimentation and innovation across diverse teams.
2. Cost Efficiency:
   - Reduces the need for hiring specialized AI

developers.
- Saves time by streamlining workflows.
3. Scalability:
   - Enables businesses to start small and scale their AI solutions as they grow.

User-friendly AI tools and low-code/no-code platforms are transforming how businesses and individuals approach AI. With these technologies, even beginners can implement powerful AI solutions to enhance productivity, automate tasks, and generate insights. Whether you're building predictive models with AutoML or creating text workflows with MonkeyLearn, these platforms empower users to unlock the potential of AI with minimal effort and technical expertise.

14. AI IN MANUFACTURING: PREDICTIVE MAINTENANCE

Predictive maintenance powered by Artificial Intelligence (AI) is revolutionizing manufacturing by enabling companies to predict and prevent equipment failures before they occur. This proactive approach not only reduces downtime but also optimizes maintenance schedules and extends equipment lifespans. In this chapter, we'll explore the concept of predictive maintenance, its mechanics, benefits, and real-world applications.

14.1 Introduction to Predictive Maintenance

What is Predictive Maintenance?

- Predictive maintenance is a data-driven approach to monitor equipment and predict when it will need servicing. Instead of relying on reactive (repair after failure) or preventive (fixed schedules) maintenance, predictive maintenance uses real-time data to determine the optimal time for servicing.

How It Differs from Other Maintenance Types:
- Reactive Maintenance: Fixing equipment after it fails.
    - Costly due to unplanned downtime and emergency repairs.
- Preventive Maintenance: Regularly scheduled maintenance regardless of actual equipment condition.
    - Can lead to unnecessary servicing or missed warning signs of failure.
- Predictive Maintenance: Using AI to predict failures and intervene at the right time.
    - Optimizes maintenance schedules and minimizes costs.

Why It's Important in Manufacturing:
- Manufacturing relies heavily on complex machinery that must operate reliably. Downtime from unexpected failures can disrupt production, delay orders, and incur significant financial losses.

14.2 How AI Can Predict and Prevent Equipment Failures

AI brings advanced analytics and predictive capabilities to maintenance. Here's how it works:

Step 1: Data Collection
- Sensors: Install IoT sensors on machines to collect real-time data such as:
    - Temperature
    - Vibration
    - Pressure
    - Noise levels

- - Voltage and current
- Historical Data: Use past maintenance logs, failure records, and performance metrics.

Step 2: Data Analysis

- AI processes the collected data to identify patterns and anomalies that indicate potential failures.
- Machine learning (ML) models are trained on historical data to understand the relationship between machine behavior and breakdowns.

Step 3: Prediction

- AI predicts the likelihood and timing of equipment failures using techniques such as:
  - Time-Series Analysis: Identifying trends and patterns over time.
  - Anomaly Detection: Recognizing deviations from normal operational behavior.
  - Regression Models: Estimating the remaining useful life (RUL) of equipment.

Step 4: Recommendation

- AI provides actionable insights, such as:
  - Alerts for imminent failures.
  - Maintenance schedules optimized for operational efficiency.
  - Recommendations for spare parts inventory management.

Step 5: Continuous Improvement

- AI systems learn from new data, improving their accuracy and adapting to evolving operational conditions.

Example in Action:

- A factory's conveyor belt system is equipped with vibration sensors. AI detects an increase in vibrations beyond the normal range and predicts a bearing failure in two weeks. Maintenance is scheduled, and the issue is resolved without disrupting production.

14.3 Benefits of Predictive Maintenance in Manufacturing

Predictive maintenance offers a range of advantages that can significantly improve operational efficiency and reduce costs:

1. Minimized Downtime

- Impact: Reducing unplanned machine stoppages ensures smooth production workflows.
- Example: A manufacturing plant avoids a 24-hour production halt by detecting and addressing a motor issue in advance.

2. Cost Savings

- Impact: By addressing issues early, companies save on emergency repairs and reduce wear-and-tear costs.
- Example: Early detection of minor defects in a hydraulic press prevents a major breakdown, saving $50,000 in repair costs.

3. Extended Equipment Lifespan

- Impact: Proactive maintenance reduces strain on machinery, prolonging its operational life.
- Example: Regular monitoring of lubrication levels prevents premature failure of gearboxes.

4. Improved Safety

- Impact: Predictive maintenance reduces the risk of hazardous failures that could harm workers.
- Example: Detecting pressure anomalies in a boiler avoids a catastrophic explosion.

5. Better Resource Allocation

- Impact: Maintenance teams can focus on critical tasks rather than routine checks.
- Example: Instead of inspecting all machines, technicians prioritize equipment flagged by AI as at-risk.

6. Enhanced Operational Efficiency

- Impact: Predictive maintenance ensures that machinery operates at optimal performance levels.
- Example: A CNC machine monitored by AI consistently produces high-precision components without interruptions.

7. Environmental Benefits

- Impact: Predictive maintenance minimizes energy consumption and waste.
- Example: Avoiding equipment overuse reduces energy costs and lowers carbon emissions.

14.4 Case Studies and Examples

Real-world applications of predictive maintenance demonstrate its transformative impact on manufacturing:

Case Study 1: Predictive Maintenance in an Automotive Plant

- Scenario:
  - An automotive assembly line uses predictive maintenance for robotic arms.
- AI Application:

- o IoT sensors monitor motor torque, arm speed, and joint angles.
  - o AI detects wear in a robotic arm joint and recommends servicing within three days.
- Outcome:
  - o Prevented a production stoppage that could have delayed vehicle shipments.
  - o Saved $$$$ in potential downtime costs.

Case Study 2: Paper Mill Prevents Machine Overheating
- Scenario:
  - o A paper mill relies on large rollers that generate heat during operation.
- AI Application:
  - o Sensors monitor temperature and vibration.
  - o AI predicts overheating due to friction from a misaligned roller.
- Outcome:
  - o Maintenance team realigns the roller, preventing damage to the entire machine.
  - o Reduced energy consumption by 15%.

Case Study 3: Oil and Gas Pipeline Monitoring
- Scenario:
  - o An oil company monitors pipelines for leaks and pressure fluctuations.
- AI Application:
  - o AI analyzes pressure sensor data to detect micro-leaks.
  - o Alerts are sent to engineers for targeted inspections.
- Outcome:
  - o Prevented environmental damage and saved millions in cleanup costs.

Case Study 4: Food Processing Line Efficiency

- Scenario:
    - A food processing factory experiences frequent downtimes due to conveyor belt issues.
- AI Application:
    - AI monitors vibration and belt tension to predict wear and tear.
    - Predictive insights are integrated into the factory's maintenance system.
- Outcome:
    - Increased overall equipment effectiveness (OEE) by 20%.
    - Reduced spare part inventory costs by 30%.

- Predictive maintenance is a game-changer for manufacturing, offering cost savings, efficiency, and safety improvements.
- By leveraging AI to predict equipment failures, manufacturers can shift from reactive to proactive maintenance strategies.
- The real-world examples demonstrate how AI-driven predictive maintenance enhances reliability, reduces costs, and ensures seamless operations.

This technology represents the future of maintenance, enabling manufacturers to stay competitive in a rapidly evolving industrial landscape.

15. AI IN LOGISTICS: BUILDING A SMARTER SUPPLY CHAIN

Artificial Intelligence (AI) is revolutionizing logistics and supply chains by enabling smarter, faster, and more efficient operations. From demand forecasting to route optimization, AI helps organizations address challenges, reduce costs, and improve customer satisfaction. In this chapter, we'll explore how AI transforms logistics, the technologies driving these changes, the steps to build an AI system, and real-world success stories.

15.1 How AI Transforms Logistics and Supply Chains

AI enhances logistics by automating processes, providing actionable insights, and improving decision-making across the supply chain.

1. Enhanced Efficiency and Automation

- What It Does:
    - AI automates repetitive tasks, such as inventory updates and order tracking, reducing manual

intervention and errors.
- Example:
  - Warehouses equipped with AI-powered robots can sort, pick, and pack items faster than human workers.

2. Real-Time Decision-Making

- What It Does:
  - AI analyzes real-time data to optimize inventory levels, manage transportation, and respond to disruptions.
- Example:
  - AI systems detect delays due to weather conditions and automatically reroute shipments to avoid disruptions.

3. Improved Visibility

- What It Does:
  - AI integrates data from multiple sources, offering end-to-end visibility of the supply chain.
- Example:
  - AI-powered dashboards track shipments, inventory, and supplier performance in real time.

4. Enhanced Customer Experience

- What It Does:
  - AI predicts delivery times, provides personalized shipping options, and resolves customer queries through chatbots.
- Example:
  - An e-commerce platform uses AI to recommend the fastest delivery method based on real-time traffic and customer location.

15.2 Demand Forecasting, Route Optimization & Efficiency Gains

AI drives significant improvements in logistics operations by addressing key challenges:

1. Demand Forecasting

- How It Works:
    - AI uses historical sales data, market trends, and external factors (e.g., weather, holidays) to predict future demand.
- Benefits:
    - Reduces overstocking or understocking.
    - Improves supplier coordination and production planning.
- Example:
    - A grocery chain uses AI to predict demand for fresh produce, ensuring optimal stock levels and minimizing waste.

2. Route Optimization

- How It Works:
    - AI analyzes traffic patterns, weather conditions, and fuel costs to determine the most efficient delivery routes.
- Benefits:
    - Reduces delivery times and fuel consumption.
    - Enhances driver productivity and customer satisfaction.
- Example:
    - A courier service uses AI to dynamically reroute drivers based on real-time traffic updates, cutting delivery times by 20%.

3. Efficiency Gains

- How It Works:
    - AI automates inventory management, warehouse operations, and fleet scheduling, streamlining

logistics workflows.
- Benefits:
  - Lowers operational costs.
  - Increases speed and accuracy.
- Example:
  - An apparel company uses AI-powered robots in warehouses to pick and sort items, reducing order processing time by 30%.

15.3 Key Steps in Building an AI System for Logistics

Implementing AI in logistics requires careful planning and execution. Here's a step-by-step guide:

Step 1: Define Objectives

- What to Do:
  - Identify specific pain points, such as delivery delays, inventory inefficiencies, or forecasting inaccuracies.
- Example:
  - A retailer aims to reduce last-mile delivery costs while improving customer satisfaction.

Step 2: Gather and Prepare Data

- What to Do:
  - Collect data from relevant sources:
    - Sales and order history.
    - Traffic and weather data.
    - Fleet and driver performance metrics.
  - Clean and structure the data to ensure accuracy and consistency.
- Example:
  - A logistics company integrates GPS data, warehouse inventory records, and customer feedback into a centralized platform.

Step 3: Choose the Right AI Tools and Models
- What to Do:
    - Select tools and algorithms tailored to logistics needs:
        - For demand forecasting: Time-series analysis and predictive modeling.
        - For route optimization: Machine learning algorithms like reinforcement learning.
        - For warehouse automation: Computer vision and robotics.
- Example:
    - A supply chain manager uses Google AutoML for demand forecasting and AWS for integrating predictive models.

Step 4: Test and Validate the AI System
- What to Do:
    - Run pilot tests to evaluate the system's accuracy and efficiency.
    - Collect feedback from users to refine the system.
- Example:
    - A trucking company tests AI-powered route optimization on a subset of its fleet before full-scale deployment.

Step 5: Scale and Monitor
- What to Do:
    - Roll out the system across the entire logistics network.
    - Continuously monitor performance metrics and update models as needed.
- Example:
    - A global retailer uses AI to monitor supply chain performance and adjusts parameters based on seasonal trends.

15.4 Case Studies and Success Stories

Case Study 1: AI in Last-Mile Delivery

- Company: DHL
- Challenge: High costs and inefficiencies in last-mile delivery.
- AI Solution:
    o Used AI to predict delivery demand and optimize delivery routes.
    o Integrated predictive analytics to estimate delivery times with high accuracy.
- Outcome:
    o Reduced delivery costs by 15%.
    o Improved customer satisfaction through accurate delivery windows.

Case Study 2: Inventory Management in Retail

- Company: Walmart
- Challenge: Overstocking and understocking across multiple locations.
- AI Solution:
    o Deployed AI to analyze sales data, weather patterns, and local events for demand forecasting.
- Outcome:
    o Achieved a 30% reduction in inventory carrying costs.
    o Increased product availability during peak seasons.

Case Study 3: Route Optimization in Courier Services

- Company: FedEx
- Challenge: Inefficient routes causing delivery delays.
- AI Solution:
    o Implemented AI-powered route optimization using

real-time traffic data and predictive analytics.
- Outcome:
  o Reduced delivery times by 20%.
  o Lowered fuel consumption, contributing to sustainability goals.

Case Study 4: AI-Driven Warehouse Automation

- Company: Amazon
- Challenge: High labor costs and slow order processing.
- AI Solution:
  o Introduced AI-powered robots for picking, packing, and sorting items.
- Outcome:
  o Increased warehouse efficiency by 40%.
  o Reduced order processing times, enabling faster delivery.

AI is transforming logistics and supply chains by enhancing efficiency, accuracy, and decision-making. From demand forecasting and route optimization to warehouse automation, AI enables organizations to build smarter, more responsive supply chains. Real-world success stories demonstrate the potential of AI to reduce costs, improve customer satisfaction, and drive sustainability. For businesses looking to remain competitive, embracing AI in logistics is no longer optional—it's essential.

16. AI IN AGRICULTURE: OPTIMIZING COW BREEDING FOR MILKING

Artificial Intelligence (AI) is revolutionizing agriculture by optimizing processes, improving productivity, and addressing the growing demand for sustainable food production. In dairy farming, AI plays a significant role in optimizing cow breeding for better milk production. This chapter explores how AI transforms modern farming, enhances milk yields, navigates challenges, and celebrates real-world successes.

16.1 The Role of AI in Modern Farming

AI empowers farmers with data-driven insights and automation, enabling smarter decisions and more efficient operations.

1. Precision Agriculture
  - What It Does: Uses AI to analyze data from sensors, drones, and satellites to optimize farming practices.
  - Example: AI identifies the optimal time for planting and harvesting crops based on weather patterns and soil conditions.
2. Livestock Management
  - What It Does: AI monitors animal health, behavior, and productivity using IoT sensors and machine learning.
  - Example: Wearable devices on cows track vital signs, enabling early detection of illnesses.
3. Predictive Analytics
  - What It Does: AI predicts yield outcomes, market prices, and resource needs, helping farmers plan better.
  - Example: AI forecasts milk production trends, allowing farmers to adjust feeding schedules and breeding programs.
4. Automation
  - What It Does: AI-powered robots handle labor-intensive tasks like milking, feeding, and cleaning.
  - Example: Robotic milking machines reduce manual labor while maintaining consistency.

16.2 Improving Milk Production through AI-Based Breeding

AI-driven breeding strategies enhance milk production by identifying genetically superior cows and optimizing breeding cycles.

1. Genetic Analysis

- How It Works: AI analyzes genetic data to select cows with traits linked to higher milk yields, better health, and fertility.
- Example:
  - AI identifies cows with favorable genes for milk fat content or resistance to common diseases.
  - Farmers can prioritize these cows for breeding.

2. Estrus Detection

- How It Works: AI systems monitor cow behavior and physiological changes to detect estrus (heat), the optimal time for breeding.
- Example:
  - AI uses wearable sensors to track movement, temperature, and activity patterns. Sudden increases in activity signal estrus, alerting farmers to breed the cow at the right time.

3. AI-Powered Fertility Management

- How It Works: AI predicts the best breeding periods to maximize conception rates and minimize calving intervals.
- Example:
  - AI integrates hormone level data, estrus cycles, and historical fertility records to create tailored breeding schedules for each cow.

4. Optimized Feeding Strategies

- How It Works: AI tailors feeding programs to each cow's nutritional needs, improving health and milk production.
- Example:
  - AI recommends feed compositions based on milk output, weight, and activity levels, ensuring cows receive the right nutrients for optimal performance.

16.3 Challenges and Opportunities

in Agricultural AI

While AI offers transformative benefits, its implementation in agriculture faces certain hurdles. Recognizing these challenges helps farmers and industry leaders capitalize on opportunities.

Challenges

1. Data Collection and Quality:
   - Accurate AI predictions require high-quality, consistent data from sensors and devices.
   - Example: Poor sensor calibration can lead to incorrect health assessments in cows.
2. Cost of Implementation:
   - AI technologies and infrastructure can be expensive, posing barriers for small-scale farmers.
   - Example: The initial investment for IoT sensors and robotic milking systems may not be feasible for every farm.
3. Technical Expertise:
   - Many farmers lack the technical skills needed to deploy and manage AI solutions.
   - Example: Farmers may need training to interpret AI-generated insights and integrate them into daily operations.
4. Connectivity Issues:
   - Rural areas often lack reliable internet, limiting access to cloud-based AI tools.
   - Example: Farms in remote regions may struggle to leverage real-time AI analytics.

Opportunities

1. Improved Productivity:
   - AI helps maximize milk yields while reducing labor and resource costs.
   - Example: Automated estrus detection improves breeding success rates, boosting overall milk

production.
2. Sustainability:
   o   AI optimizes resource use, reducing waste and the environmental impact of dairy farming.
   o   Example: AI minimizes overfeeding and optimizes water use, lowering the farm's carbon footprint.
3. Scalability:
   o   AI tools can scale to accommodate farms of all sizes, from small dairies to large operations.
   o   Example: Cloud-based AI platforms allow small farms to access advanced analytics without significant upfront costs.
4. Enhanced Animal Welfare:
   o   AI monitors animal health continuously, enabling early interventions.
   o   Example: Detecting illnesses early reduces cow stress and ensures a healthier herd.

16.4 Real-World Successes in AI for Farming

Case Study 1: Improving Milk Yields with AI-Powered Breeding

- Scenario: A dairy farm in the Netherlands uses AI to analyze genetic traits and optimize breeding schedules.
- AI Application:
  o   AI identifies cows with genes linked to higher milk production and resistance to mastitis (a common dairy cow infection).
  o   Wearable sensors detect estrus with 95% accuracy, ensuring timely breeding.
- Outcome:
  o   Milk yields increased by 25% within two years.
  o   Reduced veterinary costs due to healthier herds.

Case Study 2: AI-Driven Feeding Strategies

- Scenario: A dairy cooperative in India adopts AI to optimize cow nutrition.
- AI Application:
  - AI analyzes milk output and weight data to recommend personalized feed for each cow.
- Outcome:
  - Feed costs decreased by 15%.
  - Milk quality improved, leading to higher prices from buyers.

Case Study 3: Early Illness Detection in Dairy Herds

- Scenario: A farm in New Zealand uses AI-powered health monitoring systems.
- AI Application:
  - IoT sensors track vital signs, including temperature, heart rate, and activity.
  - AI detects early signs of lameness or fever, alerting farmers for immediate action.
- Outcome:
  - Reduced cow mortality rates by 20%.
  - Increased milk production due to healthier cows.

Case Study 4: Robotic Milking Systems with AI Integration

- Scenario: A U.S.-based dairy farm deploys robotic milking systems enhanced with AI analytics.
- AI Application:
  - Robots milk cows automatically while AI analyzes milk quality and cow health.
- Outcome:
  - Labor costs decreased by 30%.
  - Milk output improved by 18% due to consistent milking schedules.

AI is transforming dairy farming by improving breeding practices, optimizing feeding strategies, and enhancing overall herd management. Despite challenges like cost and connectivity, the benefits of AI—higher milk yields, reduced costs, and healthier herds—make it a game-changer for modern agriculture. Real-world successes demonstrate the tangible value of integrating AI into farming, paving the way for a more efficient and sustainable dairy industry.

17. CASE STUDY SUMMARIES AND KEY TAKEAWAYS

This chapter consolidates lessons from real-world AI applications in manufacturing, logistics, and agriculture. It highlights critical takeaways and provides actionable steps for implementing AI effectively across industries. These insights are invaluable for decision-makers seeking to understand how AI can solve practical problems and create measurable value.

17.1 Lessons from Manufacturing, Logistics, and Agriculture Applications

Manufacturing: Predictive Maintenance

Case Study Overview:

- A global automotive manufacturing plant

implemented AI-powered predictive maintenance to minimize downtime.
- AI Application:
  - IoT sensors monitored machine vibrations, temperature, and pressure.
  - AI detected early signs of equipment failure and recommended maintenance schedules.
- Outcome:
  - Machine downtime reduced by 40%.
  - Maintenance costs decreased by 25%.

Lessons Learned:

1. Data is Key: Reliable, high-quality sensor data is essential for accurate predictions.
2. ROI Takes Time: Predictive maintenance requires initial investments in sensors and AI models but yields significant long-term savings.
3. Scalability is Crucial: Start with pilot projects and expand once results are validated.

Logistics: Route Optimization

Case Study Overview:

- A global courier service used AI to optimize delivery routes, reducing delays and operational costs.
- AI Application:
  - Machine learning analyzed traffic patterns, weather conditions, and package volumes.
  - AI dynamically adjusted routes in real time for efficiency.
- Outcome:
  - Delivery times improved by 20%.

- Fuel consumption and carbon emissions reduced by 15%.

Lessons Learned:

1. Integration Matters: AI systems must integrate seamlessly with existing fleet management tools.
2. Real-Time Data is a Game-Changer: Accurate predictions depend on continuously updated traffic and environmental data.
3. Customer-Centric Approach: Enhanced delivery accuracy leads to higher customer satisfaction and loyalty.

Agriculture: Optimizing Cow Breeding for Milking

Case Study Overview:

- A dairy farm adopted AI to improve cow breeding cycles and increase milk production.
- AI Application:
  - Wearable sensors tracked cow activity, estrus cycles, and health metrics.
  - AI algorithms predicted the optimal time for breeding.
- Outcome:
  - Milk yields increased by 25%.
  - Veterinary costs reduced by 20% due to early illness detection.

Lessons Learned:

1. Embrace IoT Integration: Combining AI with IoT devices enhances precision and real-time monitoring.
2. Cost vs. Benefit: While initial setup costs may be high, long-term efficiency gains justify the investment.
3. Animal Welfare Drives Results: Healthier animals produce higher yields, creating a win-win for farmers and businesses.

17.2 Practical Steps for Implementing AI in Various Industries

Building on these lessons, here's a step-by-step guide for implementing AI effectively in any industry.

Step 1: Identify Clear Goals

- What to Do:
  - Define specific problems AI should address, such as reducing costs, improving efficiency, or enhancing customer experience.
- How:
  - In manufacturing: Target reducing machine downtime through predictive maintenance.
  - In logistics: Focus on improving delivery accuracy.
  - In agriculture: Aim to increase crop yields or livestock productivity.
- Example:
  - A logistics company identifies delayed deliveries as a major pain point and sets a goal to reduce delivery times by 15%.

Step 2: Gather and Prepare Data

- What to Do:
  - Collect high-quality, relevant data from IoT devices, enterprise systems, or historical records.
  - Ensure data is clean, unbiased, and representative of the problem.
- How:
  - Use IoT sensors in manufacturing to collect real-time machine performance data.
  - Leverage GPS data in logistics for route optimization.
  - Analyze historical breeding data in agriculture for AI model training.
- Example:
  - A manufacturing plant installs sensors on machines to capture vibration and temperature data.

Step 3: Choose the Right AI Tools and Platforms

- What to Do:
  - Select AI tools tailored to the industry and problem, such as AutoML for predictive analytics or AWS SageMaker for custom AI development.
- How:
  - In manufacturing: Use predictive maintenance software integrated with IoT sensors.
  - In logistics: Implement AI-powered route optimization tools like Google Maps Platform.
  - In agriculture: Employ wearable sensor technology combined with AI-based health monitoring.
- Example:
  - A dairy farm chooses AI software that integrates with IoT devices to monitor cow health and breeding cycles.

Step 4: Run Pilot Projects

- What to Do:
  - Test AI systems on a small scale to validate their

effectiveness and refine models before scaling.
- How:
  - In manufacturing: Implement predictive maintenance on one production line.
  - In logistics: Test AI-driven route optimization in a single city.
  - In agriculture: Apply AI-powered estrus detection on a subset of the herd.
- Example:
  - A courier company tests route optimization in a high-traffic urban area to measure efficiency gains.

Step 5: Train Employees

- What to Do:
  - Provide training for technical teams to manage AI systems and for end-users to interpret AI insights.
- How:
  - Train maintenance staff in manufacturing to act on AI alerts.
  - Educate delivery drivers in logistics on using AI-powered route suggestions.
  - Equip farmers with knowledge to use AI-driven health monitoring tools effectively.
- Example:
  - A logistics firm trains drivers on new navigation systems powered by AI.

Step 6: Scale and Monitor

- What to Do:
  - Expand AI deployment across the organization while continuously monitoring its performance.
- How:
  - In manufacturing: Extend predictive maintenance to all production lines.
  - In logistics: Roll out AI route optimization nationwide.

- o In agriculture: Use AI for breeding, feeding, and health monitoring across all livestock.
- Example:
  - o A dairy cooperative scales its AI system to multiple farms after successful pilot tests.

Key Takeaways

1. Start Small, Scale Strategically:
   - o Pilot projects provide valuable insights, minimize risks, and build confidence before scaling.
2. Data is the Foundation:
   - o High-quality, relevant data is critical for AI success. Investing in robust data collection systems pays off in the long run.
3. Cross-Functional Collaboration is Essential:
   - o Effective AI implementation requires input from technical teams, domain experts, and end-users.
4. Monitor and Iterate:
   - o Continuous monitoring and iterative improvements ensure AI systems stay aligned with goals and deliver consistent value.
5. Focus on ROI:
   - o Evaluate AI projects based on measurable outcomes, such as cost savings, productivity gains, and customer satisfaction.

By learning from real-world successes and following these practical steps, organizations across industries can unlock the transformative potential of AI and build a smarter, more efficient future.

18. CONCLUSION: WHY AI? A ROADMAP FOR DECISION-MAKERS

As Artificial Intelligence (AI) continues to transform industries and redefine possibilities, its importance for businesses and decision-makers cannot be overstated. This chapter consolidates the insights shared throughout the book, offering a clear roadmap for leveraging AI effectively. Whether you are beginning your AI journey or refining your strategy, this conclusion equips you with actionable steps to make AI work for your business.

18.1 Recap: Why AI Matters to You and Your Business

AI is no longer a futuristic concept—it is a practical tool reshaping how businesses operate, innovate, and compete. Its ability to analyze vast amounts of data, automate processes, and generate actionable insights makes it a critical asset for decision-makers.

Key Reasons AI Matters:

1. Enhanced Decision-Making:
    - AI empowers leaders to make informed decisions using predictive analytics and real-time insights.
    - Example: Manufacturers can anticipate equipment failures, preventing costly downtime.
2. Increased Efficiency:
    - Automation of repetitive tasks reduces costs and allows employees to focus on higher-value activities.
    - Example: Logistics companies optimize delivery routes, saving fuel and time.
3. Personalized Customer Experiences:
    - AI enables tailored interactions, boosting customer satisfaction and loyalty.
    - Example: Retailers use AI to recommend products based on individual preferences.
4. Competitive Advantage:
    - Early adopters of AI gain an edge by innovating faster and responding to market changes more effectively.
    - Example: A dairy farm using AI-powered breeding cycles produces more milk and outpaces competitors.
5. Sustainability and Scalability:
    - AI optimizes resource use, reducing waste and enabling scalable operations.
    - Example: Farmers use AI to minimize overfeeding and water usage.

18.2 Key Takeaways for Starting and Succeeding with AI

Building a successful AI strategy requires careful planning, collaboration, and execution. Here are the most important takeaways for decision-makers:

ARTIFICIAL INTELLIGENCE

a. Start with Clear Objectives

- What It Means:
    - Identify specific problems AI can solve for your business.
- How to Do It:
    - Focus on measurable outcomes, such as reducing costs, improving efficiency, or enhancing customer experiences.
- Example:
    - A logistics company targets a 20% reduction in delivery times using AI-powered route optimization.

b. Build a Strong Data Foundation

- What It Means:
    - AI depends on high-quality, relevant data to deliver accurate results.
- How to Do It:
    - Invest in IoT devices, sensors, and data collection systems.
    - Regularly clean and update your datasets to maintain reliability.
- Example:
    - A manufacturing plant installs sensors on equipment to collect real-time performance data for predictive maintenance.

c. Choose the Right Tools and Partners

- What It Means:
    - Select AI platforms and vendors that align with your needs and capabilities.
- How to Do It:
    - Evaluate tools based on ease of use, scalability, and integration potential.
- Example:
    - A retail company uses AWS SageMaker to build and

deploy machine learning models.

d. Pilot, Test, and Scale
- What It Means:
  - Start small with pilot projects to validate AI solutions before scaling.
- How to Do It:
  - Measure the success of pilots against predefined KPIs and refine models as needed.
- Example:
  - A dairy farm tests AI-powered estrus detection on a small herd before expanding it to the entire operation.

e. Foster Collaboration Between Teams
- What It Means:
  - Align technical and non-technical stakeholders to ensure AI initiatives meet business goals.
- How to Do It:
  - Educate employees on AI's benefits and encourage cross-functional teamwork.
- Example:
  - A logistics firm involves drivers in the implementation of AI-powered navigation systems.

f. Embrace Continuous Improvement
- What It Means:
  - AI systems require ongoing monitoring and updates to stay effective.
- How to Do It:
  - Regularly evaluate performance and integrate new data to refine models.
- Example:
  - A retailer updates its recommendation engine with seasonal sales data to improve accuracy.

18.3. Final Thoughts and Next Steps

AI is not just a tool; it is a transformative force that can unlock unprecedented opportunities for businesses across industries. By embracing AI, decision-makers position their organizations for long-term success in a rapidly evolving landscape.

Key Considerations Moving Forward:

1. Adopt a Growth Mindset:
    - View AI as a journey rather than a one-time project. Success requires ongoing learning, adaptation, and investment.
    - Example: A manufacturing company gradually expands its AI initiatives from predictive maintenance to quality control and supply chain optimization.
2. Prioritize Ethics and Responsibility:
    - Ensure your AI systems are fair, transparent, and compliant with regulations.
    - Example: A financial institution uses explainable AI models to maintain customer trust in credit scoring decisions.
3. Prepare for Change:
    - AI adoption may require cultural and operational shifts within your organization.
    - Communicate the value of AI to stakeholders and address concerns proactively.
    - Example: A logistics firm trains its workforce to use AI tools effectively, reducing resistance to change.

Next Steps for Decision-Makers:

- Evaluate Readiness: Assess your organization's current

capabilities, including data availability, infrastructure, and expertise.
- Create a Roadmap: Develop a phased approach for implementing AI, starting with high-impact use cases.
- Collaborate with Experts: Partner with AI vendors, consultants, or academic institutions to bridge knowledge gaps.
- Monitor Trends: Stay updated on AI advancements to identify emerging opportunities.

AI is more than a technology; it is a strategic advantage. By starting with clear goals, investing in the right tools, and fostering collaboration, decision-makers can harness AI's potential to drive innovation, efficiency, and growth. As you move forward, remember that the journey to AI success is one of continuous learning and adaptation.

THE FINAL WORD

This book serves as your guide to understanding and leveraging AI in the decision-making process. Whether in manufacturing, logistics, agriculture, or beyond, the principles and strategies discussed here will help you navigate the complexities of AI and unlock its full potential. The time to act is now—AI is not just the future; it is the present. Take the first step, and let AI transform your business.

REFERENCES

OpenAI. What is Artificial Intelligence? https://openai.com/research/what-is-ai A concise explanation of AI fundamentals and its potential applications.

IBM. What is Artificial Intelligence (AI)? https://www.ibm.com/topics/artificial-intelligence An introduction to AI concepts and real-world use cases across industries.

Google AI Blog. Machine Learning 101: A Beginner's Guide. https://ai.googleblog.com/ Explains the basics of machine learning in an accessible format.

OpenAI Blog. An Overview of Generative AI with GPT and DALL-E. https://openai.com/blog Insights into generative AI tools, including their development and applications.

NVIDIA Developer Blog. How Generative AI is Changing Industries. https://developer.nvidia.com/blog Discusses the use of generative AI in industries like media, healthcare, and design.

McKinsey & Company. The State of AI in 2023. https://www.mckinsey.com/business-functions/mckinsey-digital/our-insights Covers AI adoption trends and industry-specific applications.

Amazon Web Services. AI in Supply Chain and Logistics: Real-World Case Studies. https://aws.amazon.com/blogs/machine-learning Explains how AI optimizes logistics operations and reduces costs.

AgFunder News. How AI is Revolutionizing Agriculture: From Drones to Predictive Analytics. https://agfundernews.com Focuses on AI applications in farming, including precision agriculture and livestock management.

Future of Life Institute. Asilomar AI Principles: Ethical AI Guidelines. https://futureoflife.org/ai-principles A framework for ensuring responsible AI development.
European Commission. Ethics Guidelines for Trustworthy AI.

https://digital-strategy.ec.europa.eu/en/library A comprehensive guide to ethical AI use and governance.
Microsoft Azure Blog. No-Code AI: Tools for Everyone. https://azure.microsoft.com/en-us/blog Discusses the rise of no-code AI platforms and their accessibility.

H2O.ai. Automated Machine Learning (AutoML) for Beginners. https://h2o.ai/blog Explains AutoML platforms for non-technical users.
Gartner. Top 10 Strategic Technology Trends for 2024: AI Takes the Lead. https://www.gartner.com/en/insights/artificial-intelligence A forward-looking article on AI trends and technologies shaping the future.

Forbes. How AI Will Transform Business in the Next Decade. https://www.forbes.com/sites Predictions for how AI will reshape industries like healthcare, retail, and finance.

AI in Manufacturing: How Manufacturing with AI Can Drive a Sustainable Future This article explores how AI technologies are enhancing efficiency and sustainability in manufacturing processes.
https://www.weforum.org/stories/2024/06/how-manufacturing-with-ai-can-drive-a-sustainable-future/

AI in Logistics: The Advancing Role of AI in Logistics and Supply Chains An in-depth look at how AI is optimizing logistics operations, improving supply chain management, and addressing industry challenges.
https://www.trinetix.com/insights/the-advancing-role-of-ai-in-logistics-and-supply-chains

AI in Agriculture: 8 Practical Applications of AI in Agriculture. This article discusses various AI-driven innovations in agriculture, including crop monitoring, pest detection, and yield prediction. https://www.v7labs.com/blog/ai-in-agriculture

Ethics and Governance of Artificial Intelligence for Health The World Health Organization provides comprehensive guidelines on the ethical use of AI in healthcare, emphasizing human rights and ethical considerations.
https://www.who.int/publications/i/item/9789240029200

OECD AI Principles: OECD Principles on Artificial Intelligence The Organisation for Economic Co-operation and Development outlines principles to promote the responsible stewardship of trustworthy AI. https://www.oecd.org/en/topics/ai-principles.html

UNESCO's AI Ethics Recommendations: Recommendation on the Ethics of Artificial Intelligence UNESCO provides a global framework for the ethical development and deployment of AI technologies. https://www.unesco.org/en/artificial-intelligence/recommendation-ethics

AI in Agriculture Value Chain: Artificial Intelligence Tools for the Agriculture Value Chain This article explores the transformative potential of AI tools across the agricultural value chain, highlighting applications, benefits, and challenges. https://www.mdpi.com/2079-9292/13/22/4362

AI Ethics and Governance in Practice: AI Ethics and Governance in Practice: https://arxiv.org/abs/2403.15403

www.ingramcontent.com/pod-product-compliance
Lightning Source LLC
Chambersburg PA
CBHW071543220526
45469CB00003B/897